Holy Hub Jerusalem_s Global Impact

Holy Hub Jerusalem_s Global Impact

Maria .M

Noble Publishing

CONTENTS

INDEX 1

1 Chapter 1 3

2 Chapter 2 28

3 Chapter 3 52

4 Chapter 4 70

5 Chapter 5 94

6 Chapter 6 116

7 Chapter 7 139

8 Chapter 8 163

9 Chapter 9 186

INDEX

Chapter 1: Introduction

1.1 Introduction to the concept of Jerusalem as a "Holy Hub" and its historical significance.

1.2 Overview of the religious, cultural, and geopolitical importance of Jerusalem.

1.3 Setting the stage for exploring Jerusalem's global impact.

Chapter 2: Jerusalem's Spiritual Significance

2.1 Delving into the religious importance of Jerusalem for Judaism, Christianity, and Islam.

2.2 Exploring the holy sites and their significance in each religion.

2.3 Discussing the impact of Jerusalem as a spiritual center for millions around the world.

Chapter 3: Cultural Contributions

3.1 Examining the cultural heritage of Jerusalem and its influence on art, literature, and music.

3.2 Highlighting the contributions of Jerusalem to world culture and the arts.

3.3 Discussing how Jerusalem has served as a source of inspiration for various creative endeavors.

Chapter 4: Jerusalem as a Global Pilgrimage Destination

4.1 Investigating the phenomenon of pilgrimage to Jerusalem from different parts of the world.

4.2 Discussing the economic and cultural impact of pilgrimages on the city.

4.3 Exploring the experiences of pilgrims and their role in shaping the global perception of Jerusalem.

Chapter 5: Interfaith Dialogue and Peace Initiatives

5.1 Examining Jerusalem as a focal point for interfaith dialogue.

5.2 Highlighting efforts and initiatives aimed at promoting peace and understanding among different religious communities.

5.3 Discussing the challenges and successes of interfaith collaboration in Jerusalem.

Chapter 6: Geopolitical Significance

6.1 Analyzing Jerusalem's geopolitical importance in the modern world.

6.2 Examining the historical and current political issues surrounding the city.

6.3 Discussing how Jerusalem's geopolitical status influences global politics.

Chapter 7: Humanitarian and Social Impact

7.1 Investigating the humanitarian and social challenges faced by the people of Jerusalem.

7.2 Highlighting initiatives and organizations working towards social justice and human rights.

7.3 Discussing the global implications of addressing these issues in Jerusalem.

Chapter 8: Technological and Innovation Hub

8.1 Exploring Jerusalem's role as a center for innovation and technology.

8.2 Highlighting advancements in science, medicine, and technology originating from Jerusalem.

8.3 Discussing the global impact of Jerusalem's contributions to various fields.

Chapter 9: Future Prospects and Challenges

9.1 Discussing the potential future developments and challenges for Jerusalem as a "Holy Hub."

9.2 Exploring opportunities for further global collaboration and positive impact.

9.3 Concluding thoughts on the enduring significance of Jerusalem on the global stage.

Chapter 1

Introduction

In the tremendous embroidery of mankind's set of experiences, certain urban communities have arisen as focal points of social, strict, and international importance. Among these, Jerusalem remains as a radiant gem, its set of experiences interweaved with the otherworldly stories of Judaism, Christianity, and Islam. As a city loved by billions and saturated with old persona, Jerusalem stands firm on a one of a kind footing as a Blessed Center — a combination point of different religions, philosophies, and verifiable ages. This article intends to investigate the worldwide effect of Sacred Center Jerusalem, digging into multi-layered aspects rise above strict limits and reverberation across the archives of time.

Jerusalem's holiness is profoundly imbued in the shared mindset of three significant monotheistic religions: Judaism, Christianity, and Islam. For Jews, it is the timeless city, the sacrosanct site of the First and Second Sanctuaries, and the persevering through image of the Guaranteed Land. In Christianity, Jerusalem gives testimony regarding critical occasions in the existence of Jesus Christ, from the Last Dinner to the execution and restoration. In the mean time, Islam perceives Jerusalem as the third holiest city after Mecca and Medina, with the Vault of the Stone and Al-Aqsa Mosque filling in as essential milestones in the Islamic confidence.

Past its strict importance, Heavenly Center point Jerusalem plays had a crucial impact in molding the international scene of the Center East. The city has been a lasting point of convergence of pressure and struggle, mirroring the perplexing interaction of public, strict, and social personalities. The Israeli-Palestinian struggle, with Jerusalem at its heart, highlights the international ramifications of the city's challenged status. The journey for command over Jerusalem has been a main thrust behind territorial elements, impacting partnerships, discussions, and strategic endeavors for quite a long time.

Jerusalem's worldwide effect isn't restricted to the domain of international relations; it stretches out to social and scholarly circles, cultivating a rich embroidery of customs, workmanship, and thought. The Old City, an UNESCO World Legacy site, embodies centuries of human innovativeness and development. Its complex roads are decorated with compositional wonders, from the Western Wall to the Congregation of the Heavenly Catacomb, each a demonstration of the different social impacts that have molded the city over the ages.

Besides, Heavenly Center point Jerusalem has filled in as a cauldron for philosophical and religious talk, leading to significant reflections on the idea of presence, ethical quality, and the heavenly. The works of researchers, spiritualists, and thinkers who have crossed the city's holy areas reverberation through time, making a permanent imprint on the scholarly history of humankind.

The effect of Jerusalem resonates across landmasses through the journeys of adherents and the interest of researchers, specialists, and searchers of truth. Explorers from various corners of the globe leave on excursions to Jerusalem, looking for profound comfort and an association with the heavenly. The city's attractive force reaches out past strict affiliations, drawing people who are spellbound by its authentic extravagance, structural magnificence, and the mysterious quality that swarms its roads.

In the domain of worldwide tact, Blessed Center Jerusalem has been a point of convergence for political undertakings and harmony drives. The city's importance requires its thought in any conversation pointed toward settling local contentions and cultivating understanding among different networks. The intricacies of concurrence in Jerusalem act as a microcosm of more extensive worldwide difficulties connected with strict pluralism, social variety, and the quest for enduring harmony.

Jerusalem's impact isn't bound to the unmistakable designs that embellish its scene; it exudes from the elusive domain of thoughts and convictions that have developed and prospered inside its walls. The city fills in as a gathering ground for philosophical discoursed and interfaith trades, cultivating discussions that rise above the limits of strict doctrine. In a period set apart by expanding worldwide interconnectedness, Heavenly Center Jerusalem remains as an image of the common human legacy and the aggregate desires for concordance and understanding.

As we explore the mind boggling snare of Jerusalem's worldwide effect, it is basic to recognize the difficulties that have emerged from its challenged status. The contending cases to the city, combined with verifiable complaints and political intricacies, have added to an unstable climate that tests the strength of conjunction. However, inside this pot of strain and hardship, there exists the potential for exchange, understanding, and compromise — a demonstration of the persevering through trust that radiates from Sacred Center Jerusalem.

The compositional loftiness of Jerusalem's strict locales mirrors the yearnings of humankind to rise above the ordinary and interface with the heavenly. The Western Wall, remaining as a leftover of the old Jewish Sanctuary, fills in as an unmistakable connection to the scriptural past, where petitioners combine to offer supplications and look for comfort. The Congregation of the Heavenly Catacomb, enveloping the site of Jesus Christ's execution and entombment, is a holy space for Christians around the world, encapsulating the focal precepts of their confidence.

In the core of the Old City, the Vault of the Stone ascents magnificently, its brilliant vault an image of Islamic engineering and a demonstration of the otherworldly importance joined to the site. The Al-Aqsa Mosque, contiguous the Vault of the Stone, is a respected spot of love for Muslims, its set of experiences interlaced with the Prophet Muhammad's Night Process. These designs, each with its particular social and strict reverberation, aggregately add to the rich embroidered artwork that characterizes Blessed Center point Jerusalem.

Jerusalem's design legacy isn't only a remnant of the past; it is an honest, living demonstration of the perseverance and the flexibility of human soul notwithstanding misfortune. The fastidious craftsmanship, mind boggling plans, and the social combination clear in these designs exemplify the city's capacity to retain and mirror the assorted impacts that have formed its personality throughout the long term.

Past the actual designs, Jerusalem's roads and back streets bear the engravings of innumerable strides — pioneers, researchers, heros, and merchants who have crossed its ways. The city's set of experiences is scratched in the ragged stones and endured walls, describing stories of win and misfortune, concurrence and struggle. Each edge of Jerusalem reverberations with the murmurs of the past, welcoming thought on the recurrent idea of mankind's set of experiences and the enduring journey for importance and reason.

The effect of Heavenly Center point Jerusalem stretches out past its actual limits, penetrating the domains of writing, craftsmanship, and music. Endless artists and journalists have been enlivened by the city's persona, meshing its substance into the texture of their innovative articulations. Craftsmen, enthralled by the transaction of light and shadow on Jerusalem's old stones, have looked to catch the city's extraordinary magnificence on material. Artists, attracted to the melodic reverberations of petition and psalms, have made orchestras that give proper respect to the otherworldly reverberation of the Heavenly Center.

In the domain of writing, Jerusalem has been a lasting wellspring of motivation, its roads and tourist spots becoming illustrations for existential missions and profound excursions. Journalists, going from Nobel laureates to arising voices, have tried to catch the intricacy of the city's character and the significant effect it has on the people who cross its back streets. Through the composed word, Jerusalem rises above its actual limits, turning into an image of all inclusive subjects — trust, yearning, and the perpetual quest for significance.

Imaginative portrayals of Jerusalem flourish, each material and figure mirroring the craftsman's understanding of the city's persona. The exchange of varieties, the juxtaposition of light and haziness, and the careful scrupulousness act as articulations of the significant feelings evoked by Heavenly Center point Jerusalem. These imaginative manifestations, showed in displays and galleries around the world, act as windows into the aggregate creative mind that Jerusalem has mixed all through the ages.

Music, with its capacity to summon feelings and rise above phonetic hindrances, has been a strong medium through which Jerusalem's effect resounds internationally. Authors, drawing motivation from the hallowed serenades and tunes that reverberation through the city's strict destinations, have formed ensembles and oratorios that honor Jerusalem's profound importance. These melodic sytheses, acted in show corridors and houses of God, act as a demonstration of the persevering through impact of Blessed Center Jerusalem on the imaginative articulations of mankind.

As we consider the worldwide effect of Blessed Center point Jerusalem, it is fundamental to recognize the difficulties that have emerged from its challenged status. The city's set of experiences is defaced by times of contention, success, and uprooting, each leaving scars on the aggregate memory of its occupants. The Israeli-Palestinian clash, with Jerusalem at its focal point, has been a wellspring of persevering through strain, opposing simple goal and propagating patterns of viciousness and doubt.

The political intricacies encompassing Jerusalem are entwined with well established authentic complaints, contending public accounts, and the more extensive international elements of the Center East. The city's importance to numerous strict networks adds one more layer of intricacy, as each tries to declare its authentic and profound association with the holy locales inside its walls. The complexities of sway, access, and command over Jerusalem's heavenly locales stay vital to the more extensive difficulties of accomplishing an enduring and evenhanded goal to the Israeli-Palestinian clash.

The worldwide effect of Heavenly Center point Jerusalem is, in this way, indistinguishable from the continuous journey for harmony and solidness in the locale. Strategic endeavors, harmony drives, and exchanges keep on wrestling with the intricacies of Jerusalem's challenged status, trying to address the goals and worries of all gatherings included. The global local area, perceiving the representative and strict significance of the city, plays had a vital impact in working with discourse and interceding questions to advance a fair and enduring goal.

Notwithstanding these difficulties, Blessed Center Jerusalem stays an encouraging sign — where the desires for harmony, conjunction, and grasping persevere in spite of the wild history that encompasses it. The city's strength, reflected in the getting through presence of its strict networks and the faithfulness of its occupants, fills in as a demonstration of the human ability to produce associations and construct spans even in the most difficult conditions.

The effect of Heavenly Center point Jerusalem on the worldwide stage isn't restricted to the political and strict domains; it reaches out to the domains of training, grant, and multifaceted comprehension. Scholarly organizations and exploration focuses overall draw in with the complex elements of Jerusalem, leading examinations that investigate its verifiable, social, and strict importance. Researchers from different disciplines add to a developing group of information that tries to disentangle the intricacies of Jerusalem's at various times, cultivating a more profound comprehension of its worldwide effect.

Instructive drives based on Jerusalem furnish understudies and specialists with chances to draw in with the city's rich history and various social legacy. Concentrate on programs, archeological unearthings, and social trades offer roads for people to submerge themselves in the intricacies of Heavenly Center Jerusalem, rising above geological limits to associate with the city's significant heritage. The quest for information about Jerusalem turns into an extension that traverses distinctions, cultivating a common perspective of the city's importance among researchers and understudies around the world.

Jerusalem's effect on training isn't restricted to scholastic pursuits; it stretches out to the more extensive domain of social trade and discourse. Instructive foundations in Jerusalem, filling in as hatcheries of naturally suspected and focuses of learning, assume an essential part in sustaining the up and coming age of pioneers, researchers, and peacemakers. The encounters of understudies concentrating on in Jerusalem, presented to the city's rich embroidery of history and variety, add to a worldwide organization of people who convey the examples of Blessed Center Jerusalem into their particular fields of try.

The worldwide effect of Heavenly Center point Jerusalem is additionally intensified from the perspective of the travel industry, as a large number of guests from around the world leave on journeys and social excursions to the city. Explorers, looking for otherworldly edification and an association with their separate religions, navigate the consecrated locales of Jerusalem, each step reverberating with the long stretches of commitment that have gone before them. The travel industry, interweaved with the city's social and strict legacy, adds to the worldwide spread of Jerusalem's effect, making it available to people from assorted foundations and viewpoints.

The convergence of sightseers carries with it monetary open doors and difficulties, as the sensitive harmony among protection and improvement turns into a point of convergence for the city's specialists.

The obligation to defend Jerusalem's social and verifiable fortunes while taking special care of the requirements of a developing number of guests highlights the worldwide ramifications of overseeing Heavenly Center point Jerusalem. Manageable the travel industry rehearses and mindful stewardship are fundamental to guarantee that Jerusalem's inheritance perseveres for people in the future.

As we consider the worldwide effect of Sacred Center Jerusalem, it is essential to recognize the job of innovation in forming the story and scattering the city's story to a worldwide crowd. Advanced stages, virtual visits, and online assets furnish people overall with the amazing chance to investigate Jerusalem's social and strict legacy from the solace of their homes. The computerized age has democratized admittance to data about Blessed Center point Jerusalem, empowering a virtual journey for the individuals who might be truly far off however in a genuine way associated with the city.

Web-based entertainment, with its capacity to interface people across landmasses, fills in as a stage for discourse, trade, and the sharing of different viewpoints on Jerusalem. The worldwide talk encompassing the city's importance, its difficulties, and the continuous endeavors for goal tracks down articulation in web-based gatherings, web journals, and sight and sound substance. In this computerized scene, Heavenly Center Jerusalem turns into a hub in the interconnected snare of worldwide discussions about confidence, history, and the quest for harmony.

The worldwide effect of Sacred Center point Jerusalem isn't static; it develops with the changing elements of the world. In a time set apart by expanded consciousness of social variety, interfaith discourse, and the basic of reasonable turn of events, Jerusalem's job as a Blessed Center point takes on reestablished importance. The city turns into a microcosm of the more extensive difficulties and open doors confronting mankind — exploring the intricacies of character, encouraging exchange despite variety, and making progress toward a practical and agreeable concurrence.

1.1 Introduction to the concept of Jerusalem as a "Holy Hub" and its historical significance.

In the huge embroidery of mankind's set of experiences, not many urban communities have held as significant an importance as Jerusalem. Settled in the core of the Center East, it has been a pot of confidence, a blend of societies, and a phase for verifiable dramatizations that have unfurled over centuries. At the center of Jerusalem's charm is its status as a "Blessed Center," an idea that rises above the city's actual limits to typify its otherworldly, social, and verifiable reverberation across the globe.

The idea of Jerusalem as a Blessed Center point is well established in its job as a consecrated space for three significant monotheistic religions: Judaism, Christianity, and Islam. For Jews, the city is the everlasting capital, where the First and Second Sanctuaries once stood and a demonstration of the persevering through association between the Jewish public and their heavenly pledge.

Christians view Jerusalem as the stage for urgent occasions in the existence of Jesus Christ, from the Last Dinner to the execution and restoration, making it a foundation of Christian philosophy. In the interim, for Muslims, Jerusalem holds importance as the third holiest city after Mecca and Medina, with the Vault of the Stone and Al-Aqsa Mosque remaining as images of significant otherworldly significance.

This intermingling of strict importance has presented to Jerusalem a remarkable and extraordinary quality — a Heavenly Center point where various beliefs meet, mix, and veer. The city's roads, washed in the brilliant tones of dusk or sparkling with the morning dew, reverberation with supplications, songs, and serenades that have resounded for a really long time. The Old City, encompassed by old walls, is a microcosm of strict variety, lodging the Western Wall, the Congregation of the Heavenly Mausoleum, and the Vault of the Stone — all inside a short distance of each other.

Past its strict importance, Jerusalem has been a cauldron of verifiable change, seeing the ascent and fall of domains, the back and forth movement of societies, and the persevering through strength of its occupants. The city's celebrated past is scratched into its stones, from the archeological fortunes underneath the surface to the notable milestones that puncture the horizon. The layers of history in Jerusalem are not simple remainders of the past; they are a living demonstration of the city's capacity to adjust, persevere, and develop.

The worldwide meaning of Sacred Center point Jerusalem is maybe most clearly depicted in the continuous Israeli-Palestinian struggle, an international problem with establishes profoundly implanted in the city's challenged status. The topic of who controls Jerusalem and its heavenly destinations has been an enduring wellspring of strain, molding the story of the more extensive Center East and impacting worldwide discretion. The international elements encompassing Jerusalem are a microcosm of more extensive worldwide difficulties, stressing the sensitive harmony between strict character, public sway, and the mission for harmony.

Jerusalem's verifiable importance reaches out past the strict and international domains to envelop its effect on human idea, reasoning, and writing. The city has been a dream for writers, a subject of thought for rationalists, and a material for specialists trying to catch its indescribable substance. The compositions of lights like Khalil Gibran, Yehuda Amichai, and others bear the engraving of Jerusalem's otherworldly and social attraction, offering experiences into the city's significant effect on the human creative mind.

In the domain of worldwide tact, Heavenly Center Jerusalem has been both an impetus for struggle and a point of convergence for harmony drives. The city's challenged status has been a thistle in the side of various discussions, with each side declaring its verifiable and strict cases to Jerusalem. Political endeavors to address the Israeli-Palestinian struggle definitely wrestle with the intricacies of Jerusalem, perceiving its representative significance as a standard for both local strength and worldwide congruity.

The social effect of Heavenly Center Jerusalem is obvious in its building magnificence, a demonstration of the imaginative undertakings of civic establishments that have transformed the city. The Western Wall, with its old stones and the intense petitions of admirers, remains as a persevering through image of Jewish confidence and versatility.

The Congregation of the Sacred Catacomb, lodging the site of Jesus' torturous killing and internment, is a show-stopper of Christian design and an objective for pioneers around the world. The Arch of the Stone, with its brilliant vault and many-sided tilework, is a famous portrayal of Islamic imaginativeness and strict commitment.

Besides, Jerusalem's Old City, an UNESCO World Legacy site, is a living exhibition hall that embodies the building styles of different periods and societies. The limited rear entryways, clamoring markets, and secret patios uncover an embroidery of impacts, from Byzantine and Roman to Ottoman and Crusader. Each stone in the Old City demonstrates the veracity of the exchange of developments that have called Jerusalem home, making a permanent imprint on its scene.

The social effect of Sacred Center point Jerusalem reaches out past the unmistakable designs to the domain of scholarly and profound pursuits. The city has been a guide for researchers, scholars, and spiritualists who look to disentangle the secrets of presence and the heavenly. The rich woven artwork of strict customs meeting in Jerusalem has led to significant philosophical exchanges, encouraging a climate where different points of view coincide and, now and again, impact.

Journeys to Heavenly Center point Jerusalem are a demonstration of its worldwide effect, drawing a huge number of devotees from around the world who leave on profound excursions to interface with their confidence. The yearly convergence of pioneers, addressing a kaleidoscope of societies and customs, changes the city into a mosaic of mankind joined by a typical journey for greatness. The common experience of navigating Jerusalem's consecrated destinations turns into a binding together string that rises above strict and social limits.

Jerusalem's impact reaches out to the domain of training, with scholarly establishments overall drawing in with the city's diverse aspects. Researchers and scientists investigate the verifiable, social, and strict parts of Jerusalem, adding to a more profound comprehension of its worldwide effect. Concentrate on programs, archeological unearthings, and interdisciplinary examination drives make spans among the scholarly community and the city's living history, encouraging a nuanced appreciation for Jerusalem's job as a Heavenly Center.

The worldwide effect of Blessed Center point Jerusalem is additionally highlighted by the job of innovation in dispersing its story to an overall crowd. Computerized stages, virtual visits, and online assets empower people to investigate Jerusalem's social and strict legacy from a far distance, democratizing admittance to the city's significant inheritance.

Online entertainment stages act as channels for worldwide discussions about Jerusalem, giving a space to different voices to add to the continuous exchange about the city's importance.

In the domain of the travel industry, Heavenly Center point Jerusalem fills in as a magnet for guests trying to encounter the union of confidence, history, and culture. The travel industry, while adding to the city's monetary imperativeness, additionally presents difficulties connected with safeguarding Jerusalem's social and verifiable trustworthiness. Finding some kind of harmony between the convergence of guests and the requirement for mindful stewardship is fundamental to guarantee that Jerusalem's heritage perseveres for people in the future.

1.2 Overview of the religious, cultural, and geopolitical importance of Jerusalem.

Jerusalem, a city saturated with relic and sacredness, possesses an extraordinary spot in the shared mindset of mankind. Its strict, social, and international significance rises above geological limits, making it a point of convergence of importance for individuals of different beliefs, societies, and countries. This outline tries to dig into the multi-layered aspects that characterize Jerusalem, inspecting its job as a nexus of strict commitment, a pot of social intermingling, and an international flashpoint that reverberations through the chronicles of history.

Strict Significance:

Jerusalem's strict importance is vital, as it remains at the crossing point of three significant monotheistic religions: Judaism, Christianity, and Islam. For Jews, Jerusalem is in excess of a city; it is the profound focal point, representing the contract among God and the Jewish public. The Western Wall, a leftover of the Subsequent Sanctuary, is a sacrosanct site of petition and reflection, drawing Jewish admirers from around the world.

In Christianity, Jerusalem is unavoidably attached to the life, demise, and restoration of Jesus Christ. The Congregation of the Heavenly Mausoleum, accepted to include the site of Christ's execution and entombment, is a journey objective for Christians. The By means of Dolorosa, remembering the course Jesus took while heading to his execution, twists through the restricted roads of the Old City, welcoming adherents to stroll in the strides of their deliverer.

Islam, as well, venerates Jerusalem. The Vault of the Stone, a notable construction with a plated arch, is arranged on the Sanctuary Mount and is viewed as the third holiest site in Islam. The Al-Aqsa Mosque, nearby the Arch of the Stone, holds significant importance in Islamic custom, being related with the Prophet Muhammad's Night Process.

This strict embroidery, woven with hallowed locales and respected milestones, changes Jerusalem into a Sacred Center — a gathering ground for different beliefs and a demonstration of the interconnectedness of strict chronicles.

Social Significance:

Jerusalem's social importance is profoundly imbued in its rich woven artwork of history, design, and customs. The Old City, encompassed by old walls, is an UNESCO World Legacy site and a living demonstration of the city's different social impacts. Its confounded roads uncover structural wonders, from the Roman-period Cardo to the Ottoman-propelled markets, making a kaleidoscope of civilizations that have influenced Jerusalem.

Structural miracles, like the Congregation of the Sacred Tomb, the Western Wall, and the Vault of the Stone, exhibit the authority of different engineering styles and act as unmistakable articulations of social personality. The juxtaposition of these designs inside the bound space of the Old City epitomizes the social intermingling that characterizes Jerusalem.

Jerusalem's social effect reaches out to the domains of writing, workmanship, and music. Artists and scholars, motivated by the city's persona, have written stanzas that catch the embodiment of Jerusalem's otherworldly air. Specialists, attracted to the interaction of light and shadow on antiquated stones, have made works of art that defy the city's immortal magnificence. Performers, affected by the melodic reverberations of supplications and songs, have created ensembles that resound with the otherworldly reverberation of Blessed Center Jerusalem.

In addition, Jerusalem's roads and markets act as fields for social trade, where different networks exist together and share their one of a kind practices. The city's celebrations, whether strict or mainstream, unite individuals, cultivating a feeling of solidarity in the midst of the social variety that characterizes Jerusalem.

International Significance:

Jerusalem's international significance has been a common subject throughout the entire existence of the Center East, forming the district's elements and impacting worldwide international relations. The city's challenged status lies at the core of the Israeli-Palestinian clash, an extended battle for power, personality, and command over the Heavenly City.

The international meaning of Jerusalem is entwined with its strict and social aspects. The contending cases of Israelis and Palestinians to the city are established in verifiable stories and public goals, making a mind boggling snare of loyalties and pressures. The city's eastern and western areas have been dependent upon regional debates, with each side affirming its more right than wrong to administer and decide the city's destiny.

Global acknowledgment, or scarcity in that department, of Jerusalem as the capital of Israel has been a quarrelsome issue, with suggestions for political relations and the more extensive Israeli-Palestinian harmony process. The Unified Countries and different worldwide bodies have been engaged with interceding conversations encompassing Jerusalem, highlighting its worldwide international ramifications.

The international significance of Jerusalem stretches out past the Israeli-Palestinian struggle. The city's essential area at the intersection of Asia, Africa, and Europe has made it a point of convergence for territorial powers since the beginning of time. Command over Jerusalem has been a sought after objective for domains and states looking for impact in the more extensive Center East, adding one more layer of intricacy to the city's international elements.

Interconnected Aspects:

What makes Jerusalem genuinely exceptional is the interconnectedness of its strict, social, and international aspects. The strict scene of the city isn't separated however complicatedly connected to its social embroidered artwork and international real factors. The Western Wall, for example, isn't only a position of Jewish supplication yet an image of verifiable strength and a standard in the more extensive international setting of the Israeli-Palestinian struggle.

Likewise, the social legacy of Jerusalem is laced with its strict variety. The design, craftsmanship, and writing exuding from the city are formed by the strict stories that have unfurled inside its walls. The Vault of the Stone, with its particular Islamic building style, isn't just a strict landmark yet a social milestone that adds to the city's personality.

In international terms, the situation with Jerusalem isn't separated from its strict and social intricacies. The city's challenged nature is an impression of the well established verifiable and strict cases made by different gatherings. Settling the international difficulties encompassing Jerusalem requires tending to the strict and social goals that are entwined with the city's set of experiences.

Difficulties and Open doors:

The complicated exchange of strict, social, and international elements presents the two difficulties and open doors for Jerusalem. The city's challenged status represents a considerable test to accomplishing enduring harmony in the locale. Contending public stories, authentic complaints, and profoundly dug in personalities add to the intricacies of the Israeli-Palestinian clash, with Jerusalem at its center.

Notwithstanding, inside these difficulties lie open doors for discourse, understanding, and compromise. Jerusalem's very nature as a Blessed Center — a union point for different religions and societies — holds the potential for cultivating interfaith and intercultural exchange. Drives that perceive and praise the common legacy of Jerusalem can act as building blocks for shared regard and participation.

According to an international viewpoint, tending to the situation with Jerusalem requires a nuanced and comprehensive methodology. Global endeavors pointed toward interceding the Israeli-Palestinian clash should consider the strict and social aspects that support the city's importance. Manageable arrangements should oblige the yearnings of all gatherings included, perceiving the different accounts that meet in Jerusalem.

Jerusalem's difficulties and open doors resound all around the world. The city's effect reaches out past its actual limits, impacting the talk on strict pluralism, social variety, and the quest for harmony in an interconnected world. The worldwide local area, discretionary substances, and associations committed to compromise all assume crucial parts in exploring the intricacies of Jerusalem's complex significance.

1.3 Setting the stage for exploring Jerusalem's global impact.

Making way for investigating Jerusalem's worldwide effect requires an investigation of the city's verifiable, social, and strict settings. As quite possibly of the most established ceaselessly occupied city on the planet, Jerusalem's foundations run profound, molding its way of life as a nexus of different civilizations and a cauldron of human experience. This outline means to lay out the system for understanding the diverse aspects that add to Jerusalem's worldwide importance.

Authentic Setting:

Jerusalem's authentic embroidery is woven with strings of ancient times, demonstrating the veracity of the ascent and fall of domains, triumphs, and social trades. The city's essential area in the Levant has made it a sought after prize for old civic establishments, from the Jebusites and the Israelites to the Assyrians and Babylonians. Jerusalem's noticeable quality is emphasizd in scriptural accounts, where it is portrayed as the focal point of strict life and administration.

The foundation of the First and Second Sanctuaries in Jerusalem hardened its status as the profound heart of Judaism. The obliteration of the Second Sanctuary by the Romans in 70 CE denoted a crucial second, prompting the scattering of the Jewish public and the start of a diaspora that would traverse hundreds of years.

All through the archaic period, Jerusalem saw the rhythmic movement of Crusaders, Muslims, and different vanquishers, each leaving their engraving on the city's scene. The Mamluks, Ottomans, and English Order all assumed critical parts in forming Jerusalem's advanced personality. The city's different verifiable layers, noticeable in its design, roads, and milestones, act as a demonstration of the congruity of human home and the persevering through significance of Jerusalem through the ages.

Strict Importance:

Jerusalem's strict significance is significant, established in its relationship with major monotheistic religions. For Judaism, the city holds consecrated the Western Wall, the last remainder of the Subsequent Sanctuary, and the Sanctuary Mount, representing the otherworldly association among God and the Jewish public. Jewish travelers, looking towards Jerusalem during supplications, express a firmly established respect for the city.

In Christianity, Jerusalem possesses a focal job in the life, passing, and revival of Jesus Christ. The Congregation of the Heavenly Catacomb, accepted to incorporate the destinations of Christ's execution and entombment, draws pioneers from around the world. The By means of Dolorosa, following the way of Jesus to the execution, is a hallowed course for Christian admirers.

Islam, as well, respects Jerusalem with significant importance. The Vault of the Stone, arranged on the Sanctuary Mount, is accepted to be the spot from which the Prophet Muhammad climbed to the sky during the Night Excursion. The Al-Aqsa Mosque, contiguous the Vault of the Stone, is viewed as the third holiest site in Islam.

The conjunction of these strict practices inside the bounds of Jerusalem makes a remarkable profound reverberation, making the city a point of convergence for a great many devotees around the world. The conjunction of temples, chapels, and mosques inside nearness underscores the city's job as a Heavenly Center point — where different beliefs cross and track down articulation.

Social Embroidered artwork:

Jerusalem's social embroidered artwork is woven with the assorted strings of human advancements that have called the city home. The Old City, exemplified inside old walls, is a living gallery of building styles spreading over different ages. From the Roman-period Cardo to the complex tilework of Ottoman designs, Jerusalem's roads bear the engravings of the bunch societies that have made some meaningful difference.

The city's business sectors, or souks, are energetic center points of movement, mirroring a mosaic of social impacts. Sellers hawk merchandise going from flavors and materials to strict curios, making a tactile encounter that reflects the city's diverse personality. Every back street and square reverberates with the reverberations of history, recounting accounts of exchange, trade, and concurrence.

Jerusalem's social effect stretches out past its actual scene to the domains of writing, craftsmanship, and music. Artists and journalists, motivated by the city's persona, have written sections that catch the substance of Jerusalem's profound atmosphere. Specialists, spellbound by the interchange of light and shadow on antiquated stones, have made works of art that deify the city's immortal excellence. Artists, affected by the melodic reverberations of petitions and psalms, have formed ensembles that resound with the profound reverberation of Blessed Center Jerusalem.

Besides, the city's celebrations and festivities act as social extensions, uniting individuals from various foundations to participate in shared customs. Whether it's the yearly Jerusalem Light Celebration or the Jerusalem Film Celebration, these occasions add to the city's worldwide social effect, exhibiting its capacity to cultivate innovativeness and imaginative articulation.

International Elements:

Jerusalem's international elements are complicatedly joined with its strict and social importance, leading to a complex and frequently quarrelsome worldwide story. The city's status has been a point of convergence of international battles, especially with regards to the Israeli-Palestinian clash. The contending cases to Jerusalem by Israelis and Palestinians have prompted persevering through strains, with the city turning into a representative standard for public character and sway.

The global local area has been effectively taken part in endeavors to intercede and track down an enduring answer for the Israeli-Palestinian clash, perceiving the centrality of Jerusalem in any thorough nonaggression treaty. UN goals, conciliatory drives, and harmony plans have all wrestled with the intricacies of the city's challenged status, mirroring the worldwide ramifications of Jerusalem's international importance.

Jerusalem's essential area in the Center East has likewise made it a point of convergence for territorial powers over the entire course of time. The city's verifiable significance and strict imagery add to its international importance, impacting collusions, clashes, and worldwide relations in the more extensive Center East.

Worldwide Effect:

Jerusalem's worldwide effect is appeared from the perspective of its authentic, strict, social, and international aspects. Pioneers from around the world set out on excursions to the city, looking for profound comfort and an association with their individual beliefs. Researchers and specialists, addressing different fields of study, add to a developing group of information that tries to unwind the intricacies of Jerusalem's at various times.

The city's social and creative articulations resound internationally, with writing, craftsmanship, and music motivated by Jerusalem contacting crowds a long ways past its walls. The international difficulties confronting Jerusalem resonate on the worldwide stage, affecting political endeavors and molding worldwide talk on harmony and compromise.

In the advanced age, Jerusalem's worldwide effect is additionally enhanced through innovation. Virtual visits, online assets, and web-based entertainment stages empower people from around the world to draw in with the city's social and strict legacy, encouraging a feeling of association and understanding. Jerusalem's story becomes open to a worldwide crowd, rising above actual limits and welcoming individuals to investigate its multi-layered character.

Difficulties and Open doors:

While Jerusalem's worldwide effect is irrefutably huge, it isn't without challenges. The city's challenged status and the getting through Israeli-Palestinian clash present deterrents to accomplishing enduring security and harmony in the locale. Contending accounts, authentic complaints, and international intricacies keep on molding the talk encompassing Jerusalem.

Nonetheless, inside these difficulties lie open doors for discourse, understanding, and compromise. Jerusalem's status as a Heavenly Center point gives a shared belief to interfaith and intercultural commitment. Drives that praise the city's common legacy and advance social trade can add to encouraging shared regard and participation.

Worldwide endeavors pointed toward intervening the Israeli-Palestinian clash should perceive the centrality of Jerusalem in any far reaching nonaggression treaty. Tending to the city's challenged status requires a nuanced and comprehensive methodology that regards the strict and social desires of all gatherings included.

Investigating Jerusalem's worldwide effect requires a complete assessment of the city's verifiable, social, strict, and international aspects. As a city loved by three significant monotheistic religions — Judaism, Christianity, and Islam — Jerusalem stands firm on an interesting footing as a Sacred Center point, drawing in explorers, researchers, and people looking for profound association from around the world. This investigation digs into the complex manners by which Jerusalem's impact expands internationally, molding stories, cultivating social trade, and adding to the talk on harmony and concurrence.

Strict Reverberation:

At the core of Jerusalem's worldwide effect is its significant strict reverberation. The city's importance for Judaism, Christianity, and Islam makes it a profound focus that rises above public lines. For Jews, Jerusalem is the timeless capital, an image of their verifiable association with the land and the hallowed site of the Western Wall, where petitions to God are intensely advertised. The city's relationship with the Sanctuaries of Solomon further highlights its fundamental job in Jewish confidence and personality.

In Christianity, Jerusalem is a living demonstration of the life, demise, and revival of Jesus Christ. Pioneers run to the Congregation of the Heavenly Catacomb, accepted to house the destinations of Christ's execution and internment. The By means of Dolorosa, the way Jesus is accepted to have strolled while heading to his execution, is a journey course that navigates the restricted roads of the Old City, offering devotees an unmistakable association with the occasions of the Energy.

Islam, as well, respects Jerusalem. The Arch of the Stone, with its notorious brilliant vault, is arranged on the Sanctuary Mount and is accepted to be the spot from which the Prophet Muhammad rose to the sky during the Night Excursion. The Al-Aqsa Mosque, nearby the Vault of the Stone, is viewed as the third holiest site in Islam. The strict meaning of these locales changes Jerusalem into a sacrosanct space, drawing devotees from different social and geological foundations.

The worldwide effect of Jerusalem's strict reverberation reaches out past the actual presence of admirers inside its walls. It appears in the requests expressed in temples, chapels, and mosques around the world, as people turn towards the Blessed City in snapshots of reflection and commitment. Jerusalem turns into a binding together power, a mark of combination for the otherworldly desires of millions, encouraging a common feeling of association among different strict networks across the globe.

Social Junction:

Jerusalem's status as a Blessed Center is similarly appeared in its job as a social junction. The Old City, encompassed by old walls, is a living demonstration of the different civilizations that have transformed the city. The design, markets, and customs inside the Old City mirror the mixture of Roman, Byzantine, Islamic, and Crusader impacts, making a rich embroidery of social variety.

The business sectors, or souks, are energetic centers of social trade, where sellers hawk merchandise going from flavors and materials to strict relics. This clamoring air exemplifies the pith of Jerusalem as a spot where societies cross, entwine, and coincide. The mixing of culinary customs, creative articulations, and day to day ceremonies inside the Old City turns into a microcosm of the worldwide combination that describes Jerusalem's social effect.

Past its actual scene, Jerusalem's social impact stretches out to writing, workmanship, and music. Artists and essayists, enamored by the city's persona, have written stanzas that reverberate with perusers around the world. Specialists, enlivened by the interaction of light and shadow on antiquated stones, have made works that catch the general magnificence and meaning of Jerusalem. Performers, drawing from the melodic reverberations of supplications and songs, make music that rises above social limits, offering a sonic encounter that resounds internationally.

Jerusalem's celebrations and festivities further intensify its social effect on the worldwide stage. Whether it's the Celebration of Light, exhibiting the city enlightened in creative presentations, or the Jerusalem Film Celebration, which brings producers from different foundations, these occasions add to the city's way of life as a social center point. They act as stages for the trading of thoughts, cultivating a worldwide appreciation for Jerusalem's social extravagance.

International Importance:

Jerusalem's worldwide effect is certainly formed by its international importance, especially with regards to the Israeli-Palestinian clash. The city's challenged status has been a point of convergence of territorial and global consideration, impacting strategic relations, harmony talks, and the more extensive international affairs of the Center East.

The contending cases to Jerusalem by Israelis and Palestinians have brought about getting through strains, reflecting well established verifiable stories and public goals. The city's eastern and western areas have been dependent upon regional questions, with each side stating its on the right track to oversee and decide the city's destiny. The international intricacies encompassing Jerusalem have suggestions for the prompt area as well as for worldwide endeavors towards harmony and soundness.

Worldwide acknowledgment of Jerusalem's status has been a hostile issue, with suggestions for political relations and the more extensive Israeli-Palestinian harmony process. The Unified Countries and different worldwide bodies have been effectively taken part in interceding conversations encompassing Jerusalem, perceiving its representative significance as a standard for both territorial security and worldwide concordance.

The international elements of Jerusalem are additionally interlaced with its authentic and strict aspects. Endeavors to find an enduring answer for the Israeli-Palestinian struggle should explore the intricacies of Jerusalem's challenged status, recognizing the strict and social desires that are profoundly imbued in the city's set of experiences.

Jerusalem's essential area in the Center East has likewise made it a point of convergence for local powers from the beginning of time. The city's verifiable significance and strict imagery add to its international importance, impacting unions, clashes, and global relations in the more extensive Center East. Jerusalem's effect on worldwide international affairs is an impression of its job as a microcosm of the bigger difficulties and open doors confronting the global local area.

Worldwide Discourse and Strategy:

The worldwide effect of Jerusalem reaches out to the domain of discourse and tact. Global endeavors pointed toward interceding the Israeli-Palestinian clash perceive Jerusalem as a vital part of any extensive nonaggression treaty. Strategic drives, harmony plans, and exchanges wrestle with the intricacies of the city's challenged status, looking for an equilibrium that tends to the goals and worries of all gatherings included.

Jerusalem's worldwide impact in strategic circles isn't restricted to the goal of struggles yet stretches out to more extensive conversations on strict opportunity, social legacy, and common freedoms. The city turns into a point of convergence for worldwide discourse on the significance of saving social variety, advancing resistance, and shielding the freedoms of strict networks.

Worldwide associations, conciliatory substances, and peacebuilding drives all assume a part in forming the story encompassing Jerusalem. The city's effect on worldwide discourse highlights its importance as in excess of a nearby or local issue — a question of global concern resounds with individuals around the world.

Mechanical Dispersal:

In the computerized age, innovation fills in as a strong enhancer of Jerusalem's worldwide effect. Advanced stages, virtual visits, and online assets furnish people all over the planet with the chance to investigate Jerusalem's social and strict legacy from the solace of their homes. The democratization of admittance to data about Sacred Center point Jerusalem empowers a virtual journey for those genuinely far off however in a profound sense associated with the city.

Virtual entertainment stages further add to the worldwide talk encompassing Jerusalem. Websites, gatherings, and media content act as channels for conversations on the city's importance, challenges, and progressing endeavors for goal. The computerized scene changes Jerusalem into a hub in the interconnected snare of worldwide discussions about confidence, history, and the quest for harmony.

The innovative scattering of Jerusalem's story works with worldwide commitment as well as encourages a feeling of shared liability. People, no matter what their geological area, become members in the continuous story of Jerusalem's importance, impacting general assessment, and adding to a nuanced comprehension of the city's intricacies.

The travel industry and Financial Effect:

Jerusalem's worldwide effect is clear in the domain of the travel industry, where a large number of guests from different foundations leave on excursions to encounter the city's social, verifiable, and strict importance. The travel industry, while adding to the monetary essentialness of the city, additionally presents difficulties connected with saving Jerusalem's social and authentic uprightness.

Explorers and sightseers the same add to the city's economy, supporting nearby organizations, and producing business open doors. Be that as it may, the inundation of guests additionally requires mindful stewardship to guarantee the protection of Jerusalem's building legacy, archeological locales, and social legitimacy. Finding some kind of harmony between the monetary advantages of the travel industry and the basic of shielding Jerusalem's exceptional character is fundamental for maintainable worldwide effect.

Chapter 2

Jerusalem's Spiritual Significance

Jerusalem, a city that rises above the limits of topography and history, holds an exceptional and significant otherworldly importance for a great many individuals all over the planet. Its significance is well established in the strict practices of Judaism, Christianity, and Islam, making it a point of convergence for devotees and an image of solidarity and division all the while.

For Jews, Jerusalem is the holiest city, the focal point of their strict and profound personality. The meaning of Jerusalem in Judaism traces all the way back to old times, with the city being vital to the accounts of the Jewish Book of scriptures. Mount Moriah, situated in Jerusalem, is accepted to be the site where Abraham offered his child Isaac as a penance, a vital occasion in Jewish history. The Western Wall, a remainder of the Subsequent Sanctuary, is a hallowed site for Jewish love and journey, filling in as a substantial association with the past.

Christianity, as well, holds Jerusalem in high regard, connecting the city with pivotal occasions in the existence of Jesus Christ. The Last Dinner, the execution, and the restoration are completely connected to the scenes of Jerusalem.

The Congregation of the Heavenly Catacomb, worked over the conventional site of Christ's execution and internment, remains as a demonstration of the otherworldly importance Christians join to the city. Explorers from different Christian categories excursion to Jerusalem to stroll in the strides of Jesus and to participate in the holiness of the Heavenly Land.

In Islam, Jerusalem is loved as the third holiest city after Mecca and Medina. The Arch of the Stone, arranged on the Sanctuary Mount, holds extraordinary significance for Muslims as the spot from which the Prophet Muhammad is accepted to have climbed to paradise during the Night Excursion. Al-Aqsa Mosque, adjoining the Vault of the Stone, is viewed as one of the earliest places of love in Islam. The otherworldly meaning of Jerusalem in Islam is profoundly entwined with its verifiable and strict significance.

Regardless of sharing a typical love for Jerusalem, the city has likewise been a wellspring of pressure and struggle among the devotees of these three Abrahamic religions. The intricacy emerges from covering cases to similar hallowed spaces, particularly the Sanctuary Mount or Haram al-Sharif. The Old City of Jerusalem, with its limited rear entryways and noteworthy locales, is a mosaic of strict and social impacts that mirrors the city's rich and various history.

Throughout the long term, Jerusalem has seen various champions, from the Babylonians and Romans to the Crusaders and Ottomans. Every winner transformed the city, forming its strict and design scene. The layers of history are discernible as one strolls through the old roads, uncovering the consistent back and forth movement of various societies and beliefs.

The Campaigns, a progression of strict conflicts battled in the middle age period, assumed a critical part in molding Jerusalem's set of experiences and its profound importance. The catch and recover of the city by Christian and Muslim powers added to the confounding emanation that encompasses Jerusalem. The effect of the Campaigns is as yet felt in the aggregate memory of the Abrahamic religions, as they made a permanent imprint on the city's strict character.

In the cutting edge time, Jerusalem has been at the focal point of political and regional debates among Israelis and Palestinians. The foundation of the Province of Israel in 1948 and the ensuing Bedouin Israeli contentions have elevated strains over control of the city. The situation with Jerusalem stays perhaps of the most petulant issue in the Israeli-Palestinian struggle, with the two sides affirming their authentic and strict cases to the city.

The global local area has wrestled with the topic of Jerusalem's status, especially seeing the acknowledgment of it as the capital of Israel. The Unified Countries and different countries have taken various positions regarding this situation, mirroring the intricacies and awarenesses encompassing Jerusalem. The city's profound importance, combined with its international significance, makes any goal a fragile and testing task.

Notwithstanding the continuous contentions and political difficulties, Jerusalem keeps on being a guide of otherworldliness and a position of journey for devotees across the globe. The yearly parades, petitions, and customs that happen in the city highlight its getting through job as a point of convergence for strict dedication. The variety of strict works on coinciding inside the limits of Jerusalem is a demonstration of the city's novel capacity to oblige and embrace various beliefs.

The design of Jerusalem mirrors the entwining of strict and social impacts throughout the long term. The horizon is interspersed by vaults, minarets, and church towers, making a visual embroidery that mirrors the city's different strict legacy. The juxtaposition of the Western Wall, the Congregation of the Blessed Tomb, and the Vault of the Stone inside nearness is a striking outline of the city's profound mosaic.

Jerusalem's profound importance stretches out past its strict destinations to its job as an image of trust, flexibility, and the getting through human soul. The city has endured incalculable struggles and difficulties over now is the ideal time, yet it stays a wellspring of motivation for the individuals who look for harmony and compromise. The actual demonstration of journey to Jerusalem, no matter what one's strict association, is a demonstration of the widespread longing for profound association and understanding.

The city's profound embodiment isn't bound to strict designs alone; it saturates the very stones and roads of Jerusalem. The old olive trees in the Nursery of Gethsemane, the sunlit patios of the Al-Aqsa Mosque, and the holy quietness of the Western Wall all add to the elusive quality that encompasses the city. Jerusalem's profound energy is unmistakable, welcoming thought and contemplation in the people who cross its sacrosanct spaces.

The idea of Jerusalem as a wonderful city, where the natural and heavenly combine, is a repetitive subject in the strict texts and customs related with the city. The imagery of Jerusalem as a figurative scaffold among paradise and earth reverberates across beliefs, building up the possibility that the city is in excess of an actual area — it is a profound domain where the hallowed and the profane meet.

The otherworldly meaning of Jerusalem isn't static; it advances with the moving sands of history and the changing elements of the area. The city's versatility despite affliction and its capacity to persevere through hundreds of years of contention highlight the persevering through force of its otherworldly account. In spite of the difficulties that Jerusalem has confronted, it stays a demonstration of the human limit with respect to confidence, steadiness, and the quest for the heavenly.

The job of Jerusalem in encouraging interfaith exchange and understanding is critical in reality as we know it where strict contrasts frequently lead to division and struggle. The city fills in as a gathering point for individuals of various beliefs, giving a space to exchange and common

regard. Interfaith drives and associations situated in Jerusalem make progress toward cultivating collaboration and concordance among the city's assorted strict networks.

The profound meaning of Jerusalem isn't bound to the monotheistic Abrahamic religions. The city has likewise been adored in Eastern customs, including Buddhism and Hinduism. For instance, a few Hindu texts notice a city named Saketa, distinguished by certain researchers as an old name for Jerusalem. The interconnectedness of otherworldly stories across different societies further underscores the widespread allure of Jerusalem as an image of greatness.

The difficulties confronting Jerusalem in the contemporary world are multi-layered, enveloping political, social, and strict aspects. The situation with the city stays a disagreeable issue in the Israeli-Palestinian struggle, with the two sides trying to state their cases. The development of settlements, the boundary of lines, and the administration of strict locales all add to the perplexing trap of issues that characterize Jerusalem's contemporary reality.

Endeavors to find a supportable and only goal to the situation with Jerusalem frequently include exploring the mind boggling interaction of verifiable stories, strict convictions, and international interests. Worldwide associations, discretionary drives, and grassroots developments are all important for the more extensive discussion encompassing the eventual fate of the city. The mission for a quiet and fair arrangement requires a fragile equilibrium that regards the goals and freedoms of all gatherings included.

Jerusalem's profound importance is additionally entwined with the idea of social legacy. The city's Old City, with its tangled rear entryways and notable tourist spots, is an UNESCO World Legacy site, perceived for its social and verifiable worth. The safeguarding of Jerusalem's social legacy is a common obligation that rises above strict and political limits. Endeavors to protect the city's rich embroidery of customs add to the more extensive objective of encouraging a feeling of shared history and character.

The city's different strict networks coincide in a fragile equilibrium, having a similar actual space while keeping up with particular personalities and practices. The unpredictable dance of day to day existence in Jerusalem includes exploring the intricacies of interfaith associations, customs, and festivities. The hints of chapel chimes, the call to petition from minarets, and the requests at the Western Wall make an agreeable ensemble that repeats the city's pluralistic soul.

Jerusalem's otherworldly importance isn't restricted to its conventional strict locales; it stretches out to the daily existences of its inhabitants. The narratives of standard individuals, their battles, delights, and desires, are woven into the texture of the city. The flexibility of Jerusalemites despite misfortune mirrors the dauntless human soul and the resolute obligation to saving the city's interesting character.

In the domain of writing, workmanship, and music, Jerusalem has propelled endless works that catch the city's persona and charm. Writers, painters, and artists from different social foundations have drawn motivation from the sacrosanct scenes and authentic stories of Jerusalem. The city's immortal allure as a dream rises above strict and social limits, turning into a wellspring of inventive motivation for specialists looking to investigate the crossing point of the heavenly and the natural.

Jerusalem's profound importance isn't just a question of confidence yet additionally a wellspring of moral and moral reflection. The lessons and values related with the city challenge adherents to encapsulate standards of equity, empathy, and concurrence. The moral elements of Jerusalem's profound legacy welcome people and networks to rise above strict limits and work towards a common vision of a fair and amicable society.

The journey to Jerusalem, a custom implanted in the strict acts of Judaism, Christianity, and Islam, is an extraordinary excursion that rises above the actual demonstration of movement. Travelers set out on an otherworldly mission, looking for an association with the heavenly and a more profound comprehension of their confidence. The journey experience is a microcosm of the more extensive human excursion, mirroring the general mission for importance and reason.

Jerusalem's otherworldly importance is a living reality that proceeds to develop and shape the shared mindset of devotees around the world.

The city's capacity to summon a feeling of wonder, love, and lowliness addresses the persevering through force of the otherworldly experience. Whether one methodologies Jerusalem as a sacrosanct objective, a verifiable fortune, or an image of trust, the city's multi-layered importance reverberates on a profoundly human level.

2.1 Delving into the religious importance of Jerusalem for Judaism, Christianity, and Islam.

Diving into the strict significance of Jerusalem discloses a complicated embroidery woven with strings of confidence, history, and social importance. For Judaism, Christianity, and Islam, Jerusalem remains as a consecrated city, holding special otherworldly worth and filling in as a point of convergence for devotees around the world.

In Judaism, Jerusalem is unavoidably entwined with the personality and history of the Jewish public. The strict meaning of Jerusalem traces all the way back to old times, with establishes implanted in the Jewish Book of scriptures. For Jews, the city is the everlasting capital, the residence of God's picked individuals. The verifiable and otherworldly centrality of Jerusalem is embodied by the Western Wall, the last leftover of the Subsequent Sanctuary, which remains as an image of Jewish strength and a site of significant supplication and journey.

The Sanctuary Mount, or Har HaBayit in Hebrew, holds specific significance in Judaism. As per Jewish custom, it is where God accumulated the residue to make the principal human, Adam. Additionally, it is accepted to be the site where Abraham showed his unfaltering confidence by being willing to forfeit his child Isaac. The First and Second Sanctuaries, annihilated by the Babylonians and Romans, separately, when remained on this sacrosanct ground. The Western Wall, a piece of the holding mass of the Subsequent Sanctuary, is loved as the holiest site in Judaism, where admirers assemble to offer supplications and spot written by hand notes in the cleft of the old stones.

For Christians, Jerusalem possesses a focal spot in the story of Jesus Christ's life, demise, and restoration. The New Confirmation relates situation that developed inside the city's walls, giving an otherworldly establishment to Christianity. The Last Dinner, Christ's treachery in the Nursery of Gethsemane, the execution at Golgotha, and the restoration at the Congregation of the Heavenly Catacomb are attached to the geology of Jerusalem. The Through Dolorosa, the way Jesus is said to have strolled en route to the execution, navigates the thin roads of the Old City, permitting pioneers to follow his means and ponder the significant profound meaning of the excursion.

The Congregation of the Sacred Mausoleum, enveloping both the site of the execution and the unfilled burial chamber where Jesus is accepted to have been covered and revived, is a point of convergence for Christian pioneers. The congregation, with its perplexing churches addressing different Christian groups, remains as a demonstration of the common love for Jerusalem among Christians around the world. Explorers from various groups merge at this heavenly site, accentuating the ecumenical idea of Jerusalem's profound importance inside the Christian confidence.

In Islam, Jerusalem holds a particular spot as the third holiest city after Mecca and Medina. The strict meaning of Jerusalem in Islam is attached to the Prophet Muhammad's Night Process (Isra and Mi'raj), as depicted in the Quran. As per Islamic practice, Muhammad was shipped from Mecca to Jerusalem and climbed to the sky from the Al-Aqsa Mosque, situated on the Sanctuary Mount. The Vault of the Stone, a famous construction with its brilliant arch, is worked over the stone from which the Prophet is accepted to have rose.

Al-Aqsa Mosque, neighboring the Arch of the Stone, is one of the earliest places of love in Islam. Muslims all over the planet face the bearing of the Kaaba in Mecca during their day to day petitions, yet during the Night Excursion, Muhammad drove different prophets in supplication at Al-Aqsa Mosque, making it a site of otherworldly importance for the Muslim people group. The aggregate significance of these destinations adds to the getting through profound association Muslims have with Jerusalem.

In spite of the common strict meaning of Jerusalem among Judaism, Christianity, and Islam, the city has been a verifiable junction, seeing the recurring pattern of different realms and civilizations. The Campaigns, a progression of middle age strict conflicts, saw Jerusalem change hands on various occasions among Christian and Muslim powers. These contentions made a permanent imprint on the city's set of experiences, molding its strict and social scene.

The middle age time frame additionally saw the development of design wonders that have persevered as the centuries progressed. The Vault of the Stone, finished in 691 CE, remains as a work of art of Islamic engineering. Its complex mosaics and notorious brilliant vault add to the visual wealth of Jerusalem's horizon, implying the city's social and strict variety.

The Crusaders, thusly, raised strongholds and houses of worship, leaving an enduring engraving on Jerusalem's Old City. The Congregation of the Heavenly Mausoleum, remade by the Crusaders after its obliteration, turned into a critical journey site for Christians. The layers of history, noticeable in the city's design and roads, offer a substantial association with the past and a demonstration of the persevering through meaning of Jerusalem.

The advanced period has carried new difficulties to Jerusalem's strict significance, as political and regional questions have become entrapped with the city's sacrosanct spaces. The foundation of the Territory of Israel in 1948 and resulting clashes with adjoining Bedouin states have escalated the intricacies encompassing Jerusalem. The city's status has been a point of convergence of discussions, with the two Israelis and Palestinians declaring verifiable and strict cases.

The Six-Day Battle in 1967 denoted an essential crossroads in Jerusalem's new history. Israel's catch of East Jerusalem, remembering the Old City and the holy locales for the Sanctuary Mount, added a layer of political intricacy to the strict meaning of the city. The reunification of Jerusalem under Israeli control was met with celebration by some and worry by others, mirroring the profoundly imbued associations between religion, governmental issues, and personality.

The situation with Jerusalem has been a disagreeable issue in the Israeli-Palestinian clash, with contending cases to the city's sway. The Oslo Accords during the 1990s looked to resolve the subject of Jerusalem as a component of more extensive harmony discussions. Notwithstanding, the last status of the city stays unsettled, and contending dreams persevere, impeding an exhaustive goal to the Israeli-Palestinian struggle.

The global local area, including the Unified Countries, has wrestled with the test of tracking down a fair and impartial answer for Jerusalem's status. Whether or not Jerusalem ought to be perceived as the capital of Israel has been an especially delicate discretionary issue. Different countries have taken various situations with regards to this issue, mirroring the complex and profoundly instilled nature of the city's importance.

The international elements encompassing Jerusalem have likewise prompted worries about the safeguarding of strict opportunity and admittance to the city's blessed destinations. The sensitive equilibrium expected to deal with the different strict networks inside the Old City, each with its own customs and practices, adds one more layer of intricacy to the more extensive conversations about Jerusalem's future.

Notwithstanding the political difficulties, Jerusalem stays a dynamic focal point of strict life and journey. The Old City, with its winding rear entryways and verifiable milestones, keeps on drawing adherents from around the world. The Western Wall, the Congregation of the Blessed Catacomb, and the Vault of the Stone stand as famous images of the city's otherworldly legacy, inviting admirers and pioneers looking for an association with the heavenly.

The yearly parades and strict customs that unfurl in Jerusalem highlight its persevering through job as a point of convergence for devotees. Occasions like the Heavenly Fire function at the Congregation of the Sacred Catacomb, the Ramadan festivities at Al-Aqsa Mosque, and the requests at the Western Wall are necessary to the city's strict embroidery. These snapshots of aggregate love and festivity build up the mutual and widespread elements of Jerusalem's otherworldly importance.

Jerusalem's design scene reflects the interweaving of strict and social impacts throughout the long term. The city's horizon is interspersed by minarets, church towers, and the notable brilliant arch of the Vault of the Stone. The juxtaposition of strict designs inside closeness, like the Western Wall, the Congregation of the Sacred Tomb, and Al-Aqsa Mosque, outwardly typifies the city's assorted otherworldly legacy.

The Old City's particular quarters — Jewish, Christian, Muslim, and Armenian — mirror the concurrence of various strict networks inside the restricted bounds of Jerusalem. The amicable exchange of these quarters, each with its own practices and history, adds to the city's interesting person. The embroidery of Jerusalem is woven from the common history and interconnectedness of these different strict and social strands.

The Campaigns, frequently associated with their brutal conflicts, likewise abandoned a tradition of social trade and collaboration. The transmission of information, craftsmanship, and thoughts between the East and West during this period added to the rich social woven artwork of Jerusalem. The city turned into a gathering point for various civilizations, cultivating scholarly and creative improvements that rose above strict and social limits.

Jerusalem's profound importance isn't restricted to the conventional Abrahamic religions; it stretches out to Eastern practices too. A few Hindu and Buddhist texts reference Jerusalem, perceiving its profound significance. The interconnectedness of profound stories across different societies further stresses the widespread allure of Jerusalem as an image of greatness and otherworldly goal.

In the domain of writing, workmanship, and music, Jerusalem has been a dream for endless imaginative works. Artists, essayists, painters, and performers have looked for motivation from the city's sacrosanct scenes and verifiable stories. The songs of David, the verse of William

Blake, and the works of art of Jerusalem by specialists like William Holman Chase all take the stand concerning the city's getting through effect on the human creative mind.

The difficulties confronting Jerusalem in the contemporary world reach out past political questions to envelop issues of social legacy and strict opportunity. Endeavors to safeguard the city's old destinations, archeological fortunes, and different strict practices require a fragile equilibrium that regards the remarkable person of Jerusalem while guaranteeing openness for devotees and guests the same.

Interfaith discourse and understanding are pivotal parts of Jerusalem's job in encouraging harmony and congruity. Associations and drives devoted to advancing discourse among the city's assorted strict networks pursue making an environment of shared regard and collaboration. In a world set apart by strict strains, Jerusalem's capacity to act as a model for interfaith concurrence is of fundamental significance.

The journey to Jerusalem, a custom implanted in the strict acts of Judaism, Christianity, and Islam, is an extraordinary excursion that rises above the actual demonstration of movement. Pioneers leave on an otherworldly journey, looking for a more profound association with the heavenly and a significant comprehension of their confidence. The journey experience turns into a microcosm of the more extensive human excursion, mirroring the all inclusive mission for significance, reason, and profound satisfaction.

The moral elements of Jerusalem's otherworldly importance challenge devotees to epitomize standards of equity, empathy, and concurrence. The lessons related with the city stress the significance of moral lead, civil rights, and the quest for harmony. Jerusalem fills in as an update that otherworldly qualities are not bound to customs and functions but rather stretch out to the manner in which people and networks draw in with each other and the world.

2.2 Exploring the holy sites and their significance in each religion.

Investigating the blessed locales of Jerusalem reveals a rich embroidery of strict importance, each site addressing a point of convergence for the otherworldly practices of Judaism, Christianity, and Islam. These hallowed spots act as unmistakable epitomes of confidence, history, and the persevering through association between the heavenly and the natural.

In Judaism, the Western Wall, otherwise called the Moaning Wall, remains as perhaps of the holiest site on the planet. This remainder of the Subsequent Sanctuary, obliterated by the Romans in 70 CE, is situated in the Old City of Jerusalem. The Western Wall is a position of significant petition and journey for Jews, representing both the verifiable strength of the Jewish public and their persevering through association with God.

Pioneers from around the world assemble at the Wall to offer petitions, embed manually written notes into its fissure, and take part in demonstrations of dedication.

Contiguous the Western Wall is the Sanctuary Mount, known as Har HaBayit in Hebrew. This raised stage holds specific importance in Judaism as the verifiable area of the First and Second Sanctuaries. As per Jewish practice, the Sacred of Holies, the deepest office of the Sanctuary where the Ark of the Contract was kept, was arranged on the Sanctuary Mount. Notwithstanding the shortfall of an actual sanctuary, the site stays hallowed, and Jews face the Sanctuary Mount in their requests, communicating a profound otherworldly association with this verifiable and strict point of convergence.

In Christianity, the Congregation of the Heavenly Catacomb is a focal and venerated site, enveloping both the execution and the burial chamber where Jesus is accepted to have been covered and revived. Situated inside the Christian Quarter of the Old City, this congregation is shared by different Christian sections, including the Greek Customary, Roman Catholic, and Armenian Biblical Temples. The congregation's inside houses the Stone of Blessing, accepted to be where Jesus' body was ready for entombment, and the Aedicule, encasing the Heavenly

Catacomb itself. Travelers from different Christian practices join at the Congregation of the Sacred Tomb, making it a point of convergence for Christian love and journey.

The Through Dolorosa, or the Method of Distresses, is one more huge Christian site in Jerusalem. This way, twisting through the restricted roads of the Old City, honors the course Jesus is accepted to have taken while heading to the execution. The stations along the Through Dolorosa mark occasions like the judgment of Jesus, his falls, and experiences with different figures. Pioneers follow this course, stopping at each station for petition and reflection, associating with the significant otherworldly excursion of Christ.

The Nursery of Gethsemane, situated at the foot of the Mount of Olives, is one more consecrated site related with Jesus' last hours. It is accepted to be where Jesus supplicated the evening of his capture, and where Judas Iscariot double-crossed him. The old olive trees in the nursery are said to trace all the way back to the hour of Jesus, adding an unmistakable connection to the occasions of the New Confirmation. Travelers visit the Nursery of Gethsemane to ponder the otherworldly meaning of this area in the Christian account.

In Islam, the Vault of the Stone and Al-Aqsa Mosque, arranged on the Sanctuary Mount, are vital to the strict legacy of Jerusalem. The Arch of the Stone, with its unmistakable brilliant vault, is perhaps of the most conspicuous milestone in the city. Underlying 691 CE, it remains over the stone from which, as indicated by Islamic custom, the Prophet Muhammad climbed to paradise during the Night Excursion. The multifaceted mosaics and Arabic engravings on the outside and inside of the Vault of the Stone mirror the imaginative and compositional accomplishments of Islamic progress.

Al-Aqsa Mosque, neighboring the Vault of the Stone, is perhaps of the most seasoned mosque on the planet and holds extraordinary importance in Islam. The mosque's name, Al-Aqsa, means "the farthest," suggesting its area as the uttermost mosque referenced in the Quran. As per Islamic custom, the Prophet Muhammad drove supplications at Al-Aqsa Mosque during his Night Process, making it a site of otherworldly significance for Muslims. The inside of the mosque highlights rich curves, vaults, and complex tilework, mirroring the tasteful customs of Islamic design.

The meaning of these heavenly destinations stretches out past their strict and authentic aspects. They are images of personality, confidence, and social legacy, typifying the common stories of devotees across hundreds of years. The concurrence of these destinations inside the restricted bounds of the Old City mirrors the entwined idea of Jerusalem's strict texture, where various religions unite in a generally little geological space.

The complicated idea of Jerusalem's strict geography is additionally highlighted by the presence of the Congregation of the Sacred Catacomb, the Western Wall, the Vault of the Stone, and Al-Aqsa Mosque inside closeness to each other. This actual juxtaposition fills in as a visual portrayal of the city's otherworldly variety, where the consecrated locales of Judaism, Christianity, and Islam coincide inside the old walls of the Old City.

The Western Wall, with its transcending stones and the requests of the steadfast, reverberations with the authentic memory of the Jewish public. The Congregation of the Blessed Catacomb, set apart by its exceptionally old customs and the different Christian groups that offer its consecrated space, remains as a demonstration of the centrality of Jerusalem in Christian philosophy. The Vault of the Stone and Al-Aqsa Mosque, embellished with Islamic mathematical examples and calligraphy, exemplify the profound legacy of Islam.

The profound meaning of these destinations reaches out to the more extensive social and verifiable setting of Jerusalem. The Old City, with its confounded rear entryways and old design, fills in as a setting to these hallowed spots, typifying hundreds of years of mankind's set of experiences, struggle, and concurrence. The stones of the Old City demonstrate the veracity of the strides of prophets, crusaders, pioneers, and champions, making an unmistakable association with the past that penetrates the present.

The strict significance of Jerusalem's blessed destinations isn't bound to their job as spots of love; they likewise act as images of aggregate memory and public personality. The Western Wall, for instance, holds a novel spot in the cognizance of the Jewish public, representing both the verifiable association with the old Sanctuary and the cutting edge strength of the Jewish state. The recitation of supplications and the putting of notes in the fissure of the Wall mirror the individual and shared elements of Jewish character.

For Christians, the Congregation of the Blessed Tomb is an image of the revival and the focal occasion in Christian philosophy. Explorers from various sections come to the congregation to take part in customs and functions that associate them with the central occasions of their confidence. The common custodianship of the congregation by different Christian groups, frequently requiring fragile talks, highlights the significance of this site in the more extensive Christian account.

In Islam, the Vault of the Stone and Al-Aqsa Mosque are spots of love as well as images of the verifiable and otherworldly association between the Muslim people group and the city of Jerusalem. Muslims all over the planet face the bearing of the Kaaba in Mecca during their requests, yet the Night Excursion and the relationship with Al-Aqsa Mosque add to the city's exceptional spot in the hearts of Muslims. The Vault of the Stone's presence on the horizon of Jerusalem fills in as a visual marker of the city's importance in Islamic history.

The exchange between religion, history, and personality in Jerusalem is additionally muddled by the international real factors of the district. The situation with Jerusalem has been a petulant issue in the Israeli-Palestinian struggle, with contending cases to the city's sway. The political battles encompassing Jerusalem have suggestions for the administration and admittance to its heavenly locales, adding one more layer of intricacy to their strict and social importance.

Endeavors to safeguard the trustworthiness of these locales while obliging the necessities and awarenesses of various strict networks require sensitive strategy and coordinated effort. The Custodia Terrae Sanctae, for instance, is a Franciscan custodial request liable for supervising Christian blessed destinations in the Sacred Land, including the Congregation of the Heavenly Tomb. Also, the Waqf, an Islamic trust, directs the Muslim blessed destinations on the Sanctuary Mount.

The yearly festivals and journeys at these sacred locales add to the dynamic quality of Jerusalem's strict life. Occasions like the Sacred Fire service at the Congregation of the Blessed Catacomb, the Jewish festivals at the Western Wall, and the get-togethers at Al-Aqsa Mosque during Ramadan are vital to the profound cadence of the city. Pioneers and admirers from around the world take part in these ceremonies, adding to the multicultural embroidery of Jerusalem.

The sacred locales of Jerusalem are not simply relics of the past; they are living images that keep on molding the city's present and future. The protection of these locales includes an honest, sensitive harmony between the goals, the temporariness of political limits, and the common obligation of defending social legacy. The strict and social variety epitomized in these locales challenges devotees and guests the same to draw in with the intricacies of concurrence, common regard, and the quest for harmony.

The Nursery of Gethsemane, with its old olive trees, welcomes thought and reflection on the human experience of battle, give up, and the quest for divine direction. The Through Dolorosa, as travelers cross its way, turns into a strong excursion of sympathy and otherworldly association with the enduring of Christ.

2.3 Discussing the impact of Jerusalem as a spiritual center for millions around the world.

Jerusalem, with its old roads, verifiable tourist spots, and strict locales, fills in as an otherworldly focus that reverberates with a large number of devotees around the world. The effect of Jerusalem stretches out a long ways past its geological limits, contacting the hearts and brains of individuals across various beliefs and societies. This conversation digs into the diverse effect of Jerusalem as a profound focus, investigating its importance in forming strict character, encouraging interfaith exchange, and rousing a feeling of shared mankind.

For Jews, Jerusalem holds an extraordinary and focal spot in strict cognizance. It isn't just an actual city yet an image of verifiable progression and profound character. The Western Wall, the last remainder of the Subsequent Sanctuary, remains as a substantial connection to the old history of the Jewish public. The demonstration of confronting Jerusalem in supplication, known as "towards Jerusalem" (Mizrah), represents the centrality of the city in the regular routines of Jews all over the planet. Jerusalem, in this unique situation, isn't just a geographic area however a profound compass that guides Jewish love and interfaces devotees to their familial roots.

In Christianity, the effect of Jerusalem is significant, established in the essential occasions of the confidence. The Congregation of the Sacred Catacomb, denoting the torturous killing, entombment, and restoration of Jesus, is a journey objective for Christians from different groups. The Through Dolorosa, following the way of Jesus' last process, welcomes devotees to take part in an otherworldly reenactment of the Enthusiasm. The otherworldly effect of Jerusalem on Christians isn't bound to explicit tenets or religious convictions; it is likewise an instinctive and experiential association with the holy stories that characterize Christian confidence.

Islam, as well, respects Jerusalem with profound adoration. The Vault of the Stone and Al-Aqsa Mosque hold profound importance as the destinations related with the Prophet Muhammad's Night Process. Muslims overall face the bearing of the Kaaba in Mecca during supplications, yet the Night Excursion and the relationship with Al-Aqsa Mosque add to Jerusalem's extraordinary spot in the hearts of adherents. The effect of Jerusalem on Islam isn't just authentic yet in addition philosophical, addressing the more extensive idea of strict solidarity and the interconnectedness of Abrahamic customs.

The effect of Jerusalem as an otherworldly focus stretches out to the more extensive Abrahamic customs, where the city fills in as a shared conviction for shared stories. The tales of Abraham, Moses, David, and different prophets are woven into the texture of Judaism, Christianity, and Islam. The interconnectedness of these practices in Jerusalem encourages a feeling of solidarity among devotees, rising above strict limits and underscoring the common legacy of the Abrahamic religions.

Interfaith discourse, worked with by the extraordinary status of Jerusalem, assumes a critical part in crossing over strict partitions. Associations and drives situated in Jerusalem pursue encouraging comprehension and participation among the city's different strict networks. The Jerusalem Interfaith Center, for example, gives a stage to Jews, Christians, and Muslims to take part in exchange, underscoring the common qualities that join them. The effect of Jerusalem as a locus for interfaith exchange reaches out past the city's walls, impacting worldwide discussions about strict concurrence and common comprehension.

The effect of Jerusalem on otherworldliness is likewise reflected in the yearly journeys and strict ceremonies that draw adherents from around the world. The Blessed Fire function at the Congregation of the Sacred Catacomb, the requests at the Western Wall, and the Ramadan festivities at Al-Aqsa Mosque are vital to the otherworldly cadence of the city. Explorers take part in these customs, as demonstrations of individual commitment as well as for the purpose of interfacing with a more extensive local area of devotees who share a typical worship for Jerusalem.

The city's profound effect is obvious in the social and imaginative articulations propelled by its strict and verifiable heritage. Artists, essayists, painters, and performers have drawn motivation from the sacrosanct scenes and accounts of Jerusalem. William Blake's wonderful dreams, Chagall's dynamic canvases, and the songs of David all mirror the getting through effect of Jerusalem on the human creative mind. The city's otherworldly reverberation rises above strict affiliations, turning into a general wellspring of motivation for specialists trying to investigate subjects of greatness and the heavenly.

The effect of Jerusalem on otherworldliness isn't safe to the political and regional difficulties that have characterized the area's set of experiences. The Israeli-Palestinian clash, with Jerusalem at its middle, has prompted pressures and intricacies that definitely impact the city's profound elements. The situation with Jerusalem stays a combative issue, with contending cases to its sway by Israelis and Palestinians. The effect of political debates on the profound experience of Jerusalem brings up issues about the interaction between the hallowed and the transient.

The international real factors encompassing Jerusalem have additionally started worries about the conservation of strict opportunity and admittance to heavenly destinations. Endeavors to adjust the necessities and awarenesses of various strict networks require continuous discourse and cooperation.

The Custodia Terrae Sanctae, liable for directing Christian heavenly locales, and the Waqf, overseeing Muslim destinations, assume critical parts in dealing with the sensitive equilibrium of safeguarding strict legacy while exploring political intricacies.

Jerusalem's effect on otherworldliness reaches out to the moral elements of strict practice. The lessons related with the city underscore standards of equity, sympathy, and conjunction. The otherworldly qualities implanted in the accounts of Jerusalem challenge devotees to typify these standards in their collaborations with others and the more extensive world. The effect of Jerusalem, in this unique circumstance, turns into an impetus for moral reflection and activity, rising above strict limits.

The effect of Jerusalem on otherworldliness isn't bound to the Abrahamic religions; it likewise reverberates with Eastern practices. A few Hindu and Buddhist texts reference Jerusalem, perceiving its profound significance. The interconnectedness of profound stories across different societies stresses the general allure of Jerusalem as an image of greatness and otherworldly yearning. The city's effect on otherworldliness rises above strict classifications, mirroring the more extensive human journey for importance, reason, and association with the heavenly.

Jerusalem, with its old roads, verifiable tourist spots, and strict locales, fills in as a profound focus that resounds with a huge number of devotees around the world. The effect of Jerusalem stretches out a long ways past its geological limits, contacting the hearts and psyches of individuals across various religions and societies. This conversation dives into the diverse effect of Jerusalem as an otherworldly focus, investigating its importance in molding strict personality, encouraging interfaith exchange, and rousing a feeling of shared mankind.

For Jews, Jerusalem holds a one of a kind and focal spot in strict cognizance. It isn't just an actual city yet an image of verifiable congruity and otherworldly character. The Western Wall, the last leftover of the Subsequent Sanctuary, remains as a substantial connection to the old history of the Jewish public. The demonstration of confronting Jerusalem in petition, known as "towards Jerusalem" (Mizrah), represents the centrality of the city in the day to day routines of Jews all over the planet. Jerusalem, in this specific situation, isn't just a geographic area however a profound compass that guides Jewish love and associates devotees to their hereditary roots.

In Christianity, the effect of Jerusalem is significant, established in the primary occasions of the confidence. The Congregation of the Heavenly Catacomb, denoting the execution, entombment, and restoration of Jesus, is a journey objective for Christians from different groups. The By means of Dolorosa, following the way of Jesus' last process, welcomes devotees to take part in a profound reenactment of the Enthusiasm. The profound effect of Jerusalem on Christians isn't restricted to explicit conventions or philosophical convictions; it is likewise an instinctive and experiential association with the sacrosanct stories that characterize Christian confidence.

Islam, as well, respects Jerusalem with profound love. The Vault of the Stone and Al-Aqsa Mosque hold profound importance as the locales related with the Prophet Muhammad's Night Process. Muslims overall face the heading of the Kaaba in Mecca during petitions, however the Night Excursion and the relationship with Al-Aqsa Mosque add to Jerusalem's unique spot in the hearts of devotees. The effect of Jerusalem on Islam isn't just authentic yet in addition philosophical, addressing the more extensive idea of strict solidarity and the interconnectedness of Abrahamic customs.

The effect of Jerusalem as an otherworldly focus stretches out to the more extensive Abrahamic customs, where the city fills in as a shared conviction for shared stories. The accounts of Abraham, Moses, David, and different prophets are woven into the texture of Judaism, Christianity, and Islam. The interconnectedness of these practices in Jerusalem cultivates a feeling of solidarity among devotees, rising above strict limits and underscoring the common legacy of the Abrahamic religions.

Interfaith discourse, worked with by the remarkable status of Jerusalem, assumes a pivotal part in crossing over strict partitions. Associations and drives situated in Jerusalem pursue encouraging comprehension and participation among the city's different strict networks. The Jerusalem Interfaith Center, for example, gives a stage to Jews, Christians, and Muslims to take part in discourse, underlining the common qualities that join them. The effect of Jerusalem as a locus for interfaith exchange stretches out past the city's walls, impacting worldwide discussions about strict conjunction and shared understanding.

The effect of Jerusalem on otherworldliness is additionally reflected in the yearly journeys and strict ceremonies that draw adherents from around the world. The Heavenly Fire function at the Congregation of the Sacred Catacomb, the requests at the Western Wall, and the Ramadan festivities at Al-Aqsa Mosque are necessary to the otherworldly beat of the city. Pioneers take part in these customs, as demonstrations of individual commitment as well as for of interfacing with a more extensive local area of devotees who share a typical love for Jerusalem.

The city's profound effect is apparent in the social and imaginative articulations roused by its strict and authentic heritage. Artists, authors, painters, and performers have drawn motivation from the consecrated scenes and accounts of Jerusalem. William Blake's beautiful dreams, Chagall's lively compositions, and the songs of David all mirror the getting through effect of Jerusalem on the human creative mind. The city's profound reverberation rises above strict affiliations, turning into a widespread wellspring of motivation for specialists trying to investigate subjects of greatness and the heavenly.

The difficulties confronting Jerusalem as a profound focus are interlaced with the complex international real factors of the locale. The Israeli-Palestinian clash, with Jerusalem at its middle, has prompted strains and intricacies that unavoidably impact the city's profound elements.

The situation with Jerusalem stays a quarrelsome issue, with contending cases to its power by Israelis and Palestinians. The effect of political debates on the otherworldly experience of Jerusalem brings up issues about the interaction between the holy and the worldly.

The international real factors encompassing Jerusalem have likewise ignited worries about the safeguarding of strict opportunity and admittance to sacred locales. Endeavors to adjust the necessities and responsive qualities of various strict networks require progressing exchange and coordinated effort. The Custodia Terrae Sanctae, answerable for regulating Christian sacred locales, and the Waqf, controlling Muslim destinations, assume urgent parts in dealing with the fragile equilibrium of protecting strict legacy while exploring political intricacies.

Jerusalem's effect on otherworldliness stretches out to the moral components of strict practice. The lessons related with the city underline standards of equity, empathy, and conjunction. The otherworldly qualities implanted in the accounts of Jerusalem challenge devotees to encapsulate these standards in their connections with others and the more extensive world. The effect of Jerusalem, in this unique circumstance, turns into an impetus for moral reflection and activity, rising above strict limits.

The effect of Jerusalem as a profound focus isn't restricted to the Abrahamic religions; it likewise resounds with Eastern practices. A few

Hindu and Buddhist texts reference Jerusalem, perceiving its otherworldly significance. The interconnectedness of otherworldly stories across different societies stresses the widespread allure of Jerusalem as an image of greatness and profound goal. The city's effect on otherworldliness rises above strict classifications, mirroring the more extensive human journey for importance, reason, and association with the heavenly.

3

Chapter 3

Cultural Contributions

Social commitments are the different articulations of human imagination and mind that deeply impact social orders and advance the worldwide embroidered artwork of progress. These commitments length many disciplines, including artistic expression, sciences, reasoning, innovation, from there, the sky is the limit. The effect of social commitments is significant, affecting the manner in which individuals think, connect, and see their general surroundings.

In the domain of writing, societies have created ageless works that rise above time and topographical limits. The antiquated Greek stories, for example, the Iliad and the Odyssey, keep on charming perusers with their investigation of human instinct and the courageous excursion. Essentially, crafted by Shakespeare, from misfortunes like Hamlet to comedies like A Midsummer Night's Fantasy, feature the profundity of human feelings and the intricacies of the human experience. These scholarly magnum opuses act as a demonstration of the persevering through force of narrating for the purpose of conveying widespread bits of insight.

Imaginative articulations, appeared through visual expressions, music, and dance, give one more aspect to social commitments. The Renaissance time frame in Europe saw a prospering of imaginative imagination, with works of art like Leonardo da Vinci's Mona Lisa and Michelangelo's Sistine Sanctuary roof. These works not just mirror the specialized ability of the craftsmen yet additionally catch the social and cultural subtleties of their time. Likewise, the perplexing dance types of India, like Bharatanatyam and Kathak, recount accounts of folklore and custom through expressive developments and signals, safeguarding and sending social legacy across ages.

Logical accomplishments structure a urgent piece of social commitments, forming the manner in which people figure out the normal world. The Islamic Brilliant Age, traversing from the eighth to the fourteenth 100 years, saw huge progressions in fields like stargazing, medication, and math. Researchers like Al-Razi and Ibn Sina made earth shattering commitments to medication, establishing the groundwork for current medical care rehearses. In the mean time, the logical upset in Europe during the sixteenth and seventeenth hundreds of years denoted a change in perspective in grasping the laws of nature, with figures like Copernicus, Galileo, and Newton reforming the field of cosmology and physical science.

Reasoning, as a discipline, plays had a urgent impact in shaping social idea and affecting cultural qualities. The antiquated Greek rationalists, including Socrates, Plato, and Aristotle, laid the preparation for Western way of thinking by investigating central inquiries concerning presence, ethical quality, and information. The Edification time additionally moved philosophical request, with scholars like John Locke, Voltaire, and Jean-Jacques Rousseau upholding for standards of individual privileges, reason, and the quest for information. These philosophical commitments keep on illuminating moral and moral discussions in contemporary society.

Language itself is an essential social commitment, filling in as a vehicle for correspondence and the transmission of information. The improvement of composed language frameworks, like the cuneiform content in antiquated Mesopotamia and the symbolic representations of old Egypt, checked urgent achievements in mankind's set of experiences. The development of dialects after some time mirrors the unique idea of societies, with each semantic subtlety conveying layers of verifiable and social importance. In addition, the safeguarding of native dialects is fundamental for keeping up with the social character of different networks all over the planet.

Mechanical developments stand as a demonstration of human creativity and the capacity to adjust and work on the personal satisfaction. The Modern Upheaval, which started in the eighteenth hundred years, changed social orders by presenting automated creation and mechanical headways. The steam motor, the cotton gin, and later, the creations of the nineteenth and twentieth hundreds of years, like the phone, power, and the web, changed the manner in which individuals lived and worked. These innovative commitments expanded proficiency as well as worked with worldwide availability and the trading of thoughts.

Strict and profound convictions have additionally essentially molded social commitments, affecting workmanship, design, writing, and cultural standards. The development of wonderful strict designs, like the Gothic houses of God of Europe or the sanctuaries of Angkor Wat in Cambodia, mirrors the combination of confidence and imaginative articulation. Strict texts, whether the Book of scriptures, the Quran, or the Bhagavad Gita, act as primary support points for moral and moral direction, molding the social upsides of networks around the world.

Social commitments reach out past the substantial appearances of workmanship, writing, and innovation to incorporate elusive angles like fables, customs, and ceremonies. Classic stories and oral customs, went down through ages, protect the aggregate insight and character of networks. Conventional functions and customs, whether celebrating harvests, transitional experiences, or strict observances, give a feeling of coherence and having a place, interfacing people to their social roots.

The globalization of culture in the contemporary world has prompted expanded intercultural trade and the combination of different impacts. As social orders become more interconnected, the mixing of customs, foods, and imaginative styles makes a rich and dynamic social mosaic. In any case, this globalization additionally brings up issues about social allocation and the protection of exceptional social characters despite homogenizing patterns.

3.1 Examining the cultural heritage of Jerusalem and its influence on art, literature, and music.

Inspecting the social legacy of Jerusalem reveals an embroidery woven with strings of history, religion, and variety. As quite possibly of the most established consistently possessed city on the planet, Jerusalem holds a novel spot in the hearts of billions, worshipped by Judaism, Christianity, and Islam. Its social importance rises above international limits, making a permanent imprint on craftsmanship, writing, and music.

Specialists, attracted to Jerusalem's significant verifiable and profound quality, have long looked for motivation inside its antiquated walls. The city's design, a demonstration of hundreds of years of social blend, has been a point of convergence for imaginative articulation. The notable Vault of the Stone, with its stunning brilliant arch, and the Western Wall, a remainder of the Subsequent Sanctuary, stand as images of Jerusalem's strict and verifiable significance. Incalculable compositions, models, and photos have caught these milestones, every craftsman instilling their work with an individual translation of Jerusalem's social extravagance.

Jerusalem's Old City, an UNESCO World Legacy Site, fills in as a living material for specialists who track down motivation in its restricted roads, lively business sectors, and hallowed destinations. The juxtaposition of various compositional styles, from Mamluk designs to Ottoman impacts, establishes an outwardly charming climate.

The perplexing subtleties of the city's doors, the old stones of its walls, and the transaction of light and shadow in its rear entryways give vast potential outcomes to creative investigation. Since the beginning of time, Jerusalem has been a dream for famous craftsmen, for example, Marc Chagall, who portrayed the city's otherworldly embodiment in his illusory works of art.

Writing, as well, has been profoundly affected by Jerusalem's social legacy. Essayists, writers, and researchers have been attracted to the city's intricacy, involving it as a scenery for stories that investigate subjects of confidence, personality, and concurrence. Crafted by prestigious creators like Amos Oz and A.B. Yehoshua frequently mirror the mind boggling woven artwork of Jerusalem, winding around together the accounts of its assorted occupants. These scholarly manifestations dig into the intricacies of life in a city where history and contemporary difficulties coincide.

Jerusalem's part in strict texts, like the Book of scriptures, the Quran, and the Tanakh, has additionally energized artistic investigation. The city's roads, slopes, and valleys are portrayed in clear detail, filling in as the setting for scriptural stories and prophetic dreams. The verse of Jerusalem rises above the actual scene, turning into an illustration for profound longing and heavenly association. In contemporary writing, writers keep on wrestling with the city's importance, investigating the effect of its set of experiences on the present and it its future in a quickly impacting world to imagine.

Music, with its capacity to summon feeling and convey social subtleties, has been profoundly affected by Jerusalem's rich legacy. The city's assorted melodic practices, established in strict ceremonies and public festivals, mirror the multicultural woven artwork of its occupants. Conventional Jewish, Christian, and Islamic music coincide, each adding to the orchestra of Jerusalem's social character.

The hints of ritualistic serenades, whether exuding from the Western Wall, the Congregation of the Heavenly Mausoleum, or the Al-Aqsa Mosque, reverberation through the city, making an amicable mix of sacrosanct tunes. Artists from various foundations draw motivation from these antiquated melodic customs, injecting them with contemporary components to make imaginative structures. The oud, a conventional Center Eastern instrument, frequently becomes the dominant focal point, winding around tunes that overcome any barrier among at various times.

Jerusalem's job as a junction of societies is obvious in its melodic variety. The city's roads wake up with the rhythms of road artists, performing everything from traditional arrangements to society tunes. The yearly Jerusalem Sacrosanct Live performance features this variety, uniting specialists from different confidence customs to praise the widespread language of music. Along these lines, Jerusalem fills in as a dream for performers who try to investigate the common human experience through the force of sound.

Past the domains of workmanship, writing, and music, Jerusalem's social legacy reaches out to its culinary customs, customary artworks, and ceremonies that mark critical life altering situations. The city's business sectors, for example, the clamoring Mahane Yehuda Market, offer a tangible encounter that mirrors the variety of its populace. Customary dishes like falafel, hummus, and shawarma are not simply culinary pleasures but rather additionally take the stand concerning hundreds of years of social trade and variation.

Craftsmanship in Jerusalem is a living demonstration of the abilities went down through ages. Whether it be the complicated weaving of Palestinian craftsmans or the fragile filigree work of Jewish silversmiths, the city's craftspeople add to the safeguarding of social legacy. Each piece recounts a story, interfacing the past with the present and guaranteeing that Jerusalem's customs persevere.

Customs and services, from strict parades to customary weddings, give a brief look into the social texture of Jerusalem. The mixing of old traditions with contemporary practices mirrors the city's dynamic nature. These ceremonies act as a type of social articulation, supporting the securities that integrate networks and denoting the progression of time in a city where history is a consistently present buddy.

Jerusalem's social legacy isn't without its difficulties. The city, at the convergence of international pressures and strict awarenesses, has seen times of contention and removal. The continuous intricacies of the Israeli-Palestinian struggle, with contending cases to the city, add layers of intricacy to its social story. Exploring these difficulties requires a fragile harmony between safeguarding the city's legacy and cultivating a future that embraces variety and concurrence.

All in all, looking at the social legacy of Jerusalem uncovers a multi-layered embroidery formed by hundreds of years of history, strict importance, and social variety. The city's effect on workmanship, writing, and music is significant, with craftsmen and makers drawing motivation from its old walls and complex accounts. Jerusalem's social extravagance isn't static; it is a no nonsense substance that keeps on developing, mirroring the flexibility and versatility of its occupants. As the city wrestles with contemporary difficulties, it stays an image of the persevering through force of social legacy to rise above limits and interface individuals across existence.

3.2 Highlighting the contributions of Jerusalem to world culture and the arts.

Jerusalem, a city saturated with history and otherworldliness, has made significant commitments to world culture and human expressions all through the ages. Settled in the core of the Center East, it has been a point of convergence for different civic establishments, religions, and societies, each making a permanent imprint on the city's rich embroidery.

The social legacy of Jerusalem is profoundly interlaced with its strict importance. As a blessed city for Judaism, Christianity, and Islam, Jerusalem has been a wellspring of motivation for craftsmen, performers, essayists, and scholars across the hundreds of years. The city's strict variety has led to a special combination of creative articulations, mixing different practices and styles.

One of the most notorious images of Jerusalem's social commitments is the Old City, an UNESCO World Legacy site. Its limited winding roads, old stone design, and noteworthy milestones give a clear scenery to creative motivation. The Western Wall, a sacrosanct site in Judaism, has been a subject of endless works of art, catching the otherworldly pith of this venerated area.

Jerusalem's social effect stretches out past its actual milestones. The city has been a dream for writers, journalists, and rationalists who looked to investigate the more profound implications of presence. The verse of Jerusalem rises above the limits of time, mirroring the city's persevering through importance in the human creative mind.

Creative developments have thrived inside the city, drawing motivation from its assorted social and strict legacy. The energetic road workmanship scene in current Jerusalem mirrors a unique combination of customary and contemporary impacts. Paintings portraying strict themes, verifiable occasions, and cultural topics enhance the city's walls, making a visual story that resounds with local people and guests the same.

Music plays had a critical impact in Jerusalem's social story, reverberating through its old roads and present day settings. The city's assorted melodic practices, going from conventional Jewish klezmer to Arabic maqam, have impacted craftsmen around the world. Jerusalem's yearly Oud Celebration praises the rich woven artwork of Center Eastern music, displaying nearby and worldwide ability.

The performing expressions have tracked down a home in Jerusalem's theaters and social establishments. The city's lively theater scene investigates a great many subjects, from verifiable dramatizations to contemporary social issues. Jerusalem's Worldwide Film Celebration has turned into a stage for movie producers to exhibit their work, encouraging social trade and creative exchange.

Writing has prospered in Jerusalem, with authors drawing motivation from its complicated history and strict importance. Crafted by creators, for example, Amos Oz and Yehuda Amichai dig into the complexities of personality, having a place, and the human involvement with the setting of Jerusalem's novel social scene. These scholarly voices add to a more extensive worldwide discussion about the exchange between culture, otherworldliness, and society.

Jerusalem's exhibition halls stand as storehouses of its social inheritance, lodging antiques that range centuries. The Israel Historical center, with its broad assortment of craftsmanship and paleontology, gives a far reaching outline of the locale's social legacy. The Pinnacle of David Historical center, situated inside the old fortress, offers a dazzling excursion through Jerusalem's set of experiences, underscoring its job as a social junction.

The city's effect on world culture is additionally clear in its culinary practices. Jerusalem's different food mirrors the converging of flavors from Jewish, Middle Easterner, and Christian people group. The clamoring markets, for example, Mahane Yehuda, offer a tangible encounter where the fragrances of flavors, the shades of new produce, and the hints of merchants unite to make a culinary mosaic.

Past its unmistakable social commitments, Jerusalem has filled in as an impetus for scholarly and profound pursuits. The city's part in significantly shaping strict idea and reasoning is unmatched. The Western philosophical custom, well established in progress of old Greek masterminds, has been enhanced by the commitments of Jewish, Christian, and Islamic researchers who took part in scholarly talk inside Jerusalem's walls.

Jerusalem's effect on the Abrahamic religions is boundless. The city's strict texts, including the Jewish Book of scriptures, the New Confirmation, and the Quran, have formed the convictions and practices of billions of individuals around the world. The consecrated destinations inside Jerusalem, like the Congregation of the Blessed Catacomb, the Arch of the Stone, and the Western Wall, draw travelers and researchers the same, adding to the continuous exchange among confidence and culture.

The city's instructive foundations, including the Jewish College of Jerusalem and Al-Quds College, encourage scholastic pursuits that rise above social and strict partitions. Researchers from assorted disciplines join in Jerusalem, participating in exploration and discourse that add to the worldwide scholarly scene.

Jerusalem's obligation to interfaith exchange and understanding is exemplified by drives like the Elijah Interfaith Establishment. These endeavors look to connect the holes between strict networks, encouraging a feeling of participation and common regard. Jerusalem's job as a gathering point for various beliefs positions it as a signal of strict resistance and conjunction.

In the domain of design, Jerusalem's horizon recounts an account of social trade and verifiable congruity. The juxtaposition of old designs with current structures mirrors the city's developing personality. The reclamation endeavors in the Old City, saving its building legacy, highlight the obligation to shielding Jerusalem's social heritage for people in the future.

The city's celebrations and occasions praise its social energy, giving stages to craftsmen, performers, and masterminds to grandstand their abilities. The Jerusalem Celebration of Light changes the Old City into an enlightened scene, featuring the excellence of its design and making an otherworldly air for occupants and guests the same.

Jerusalem's social commitments reach out past its nearby lines, impacting worldwide talk on workmanship, religion, and personality. The city's getting through importance in the aggregate creative mind fills in as a sign of the interconnectedness of mankind's social legacy.

All in all, Jerusalem's commitments to world culture and artistic expressions are complex and persevering. The city's strict, authentic, and social importance has roused craftsmen, masterminds, and makers all through the ages. From the old roads of the Old City to the cutting edge settings that exhibit its dynamic social scene, Jerusalem keeps on being a wellspring of motivation and a demonstration of the persevering through force of social trade. As a junction of civic establishments, religions, and thoughts, Jerusalem's effect on the worldwide social scene is significant, and its heritage keeps on molding the manner in which we see and draw in with the world.

3.3 Discussing how Jerusalem has served as a source of inspiration for various creative endeavors.

Jerusalem, a city with a celebrated history going back centuries, has for some time been a wellspring of motivation for a bunch of imaginative undertakings. Its significant strict importance, authentic wealth, and social variety have by and large gave prolific ground to craftsmen, essayists, performers, and scholars to draw motivation and produce works that resound across reality.

At the core of Jerusalem's rousing charm is its status as a sacred city for three significant Abrahamic religions: Judaism, Christianity, and Islam. This holy group of three of religions unites in Jerusalem, making it a profound focal point where the heavenly and the natural cross. The strict stories related with the city, whether it be the Western Wall, the Congregation of the Heavenly Tomb, or the Arch of the Stone, have filled in as strong themes in endless imaginative articulations.

Specialists, since forever ago, have been enamored by the visual and representative extravagance implanted in the city's strict design. The unpredictable subtleties of the heavenly locales, the play of light and shadow on old stones, and the obvious feeling of otherworldliness have been repetitive subjects in artistic creations, models, and other visual expressions. Jerusalem's strict milestones, with their significant authentic and religious importance, have become subjects as well as wellsprings of innovative energy for specialists looking to catch the quintessence of the heavenly.

Writing, as well, has tracked down motivation in the embroidered artwork of Jerusalem's strict and verifiable accounts. Incalculable books, sonnets, and expositions have been written by scholars charmed by the city's extraordinary climate. Crafted by prestigious creators, for example, Chaim Potok, who investigated the intricacies of strict personality in Jerusalem, and the strong verse of Mahmoud Darwish, pondering the city's authentic and political aspects, feature the assorted manners by which Jerusalem has filled abstract imagination.

Jerusalem's twisted roads, antiquated walls, and different areas have filled in as settings for books that dive into the human condition. The city turns into a person by its own doing, forming the stories of heroes who explore its mind boggling social and verifiable territory. These scholarly investigations add to a more extensive comprehension of Jerusalem as a microcosm of the human experience, where individual and aggregate stories cross.

In the domain of music, Jerusalem's different social and strict legacy has been a wellspring of motivation for writers and performers. The city's remarkable soundscape, mixing the calls to petition from minarets with the songs of temple drones, has been integrated into melodic arrangements that rise above strict limits. From traditional structures to contemporary works, Jerusalem's sonic embroidered artwork has made a permanent imprint on the universe of music.

The Oud Celebration, a yearly festival of Center Eastern music held in Jerusalem, epitomizes the city's job as a center for melodic imagination. The celebration unites artists from various foundations, cultivating multifaceted joint efforts that mirror the amicable concurrence of assorted melodic customs in the city. Jerusalem's commitment to the worldwide melodic scene lies in its verifiable reverberation as well as in its capacity to support advancement and cooperation.

Theater, as a type of imaginative articulation, has flourished in Jerusalem, offering a stage for investigating the intricacies of personality, history, and cultural elements. The city's venues have facilitated exhibitions that reach from authentic shows portraying significant minutes in Jerusalem's past to contemporary plays resolving squeezing social issues. The stage turns into a space for discourse and reflection, where the city's diverse nature is rejuvenated through the specialty of narrating.

Jerusalem's social effect reaches out past conventional imaginative disciplines to include the domain of film and visual narrating. The city's extraordinary mix of old and present day, holy and mainstream, gives an outwardly convincing background to movie producers looking to investigate subjects of contention, otherworldliness, and concurrence.

Narratives and component films shot in Jerusalem frequently act as windows into the city's intricacies, offering crowds a nuanced comprehension of its social and verifiable layers.

The visual expressions, including painting and model, have been significantly affected by Jerusalem's particular scene and verifiable importance. Craftsmen from different foundations have been attracted to the city's old design, lively business sectors, and strict imagery. The juxtaposition of the old and the new, the sacrosanct and the commonplace, fills in as a visual illustration that craftsmen have handily integrated into their works.

Jerusalem's contemporary workmanship scene mirrors a powerful combination of customary and present day impacts. Nearby and worldwide craftsmen add to a visual exchange that tends to subjects like character, memory, and the effect of international real factors on individual lives. The city's specialty displays and show spaces give stages to craftsmen to draw in with Jerusalem's at various times, adding to a more extensive discussion about the convergence of craftsmanship, culture, and society.

Past the domains of human expression, Jerusalem has been a wellspring of scholarly motivation, impacting philosophical and religious talk. The city's importance in strict customs has started significant reflections on the idea of heavenly nature, the human condition, and the transaction among confidence and reason. Thinkers and scholars who have crossed the roads of Jerusalem add to a worldwide discourse that rises above social and strict limits.

Jerusalem's job as a middle for scholarly pursuits further highlights its effect on scholarly innovativeness. The city is home to esteemed establishments like the Jewish College of Jerusalem and Al-Quds College, where researchers take part in research that traverses a large number of disciplines. The scholarly local area in Jerusalem fills in as an impetus for development and decisive reasoning, adding to the progression of information on a worldwide scale.

Interfaith exchange, worked with by associations, for example, the Elijah Interfaith Foundation, epitomizes Jerusalem's job as a wellspring of motivation for cultivating understanding and participation among various strict networks. Drives that unite researchers, strict pioneers, and masterminds from different foundations add to a common investigation of normal qualities and desires, rising above social and strict contrasts.

Jerusalem's obligation to saving its social legacy is clear in the rebuilding endeavors attempted to defend its notable locales and design treasures. The careful reclamation of the Old City, with its old walls and milestones, mirrors a devotion to saving the substantial articulations of Jerusalem's rich history. These endeavors add to the city's stylish allure as well as act as a demonstration of the significance of social congruity and safeguarding.

All in all, Jerusalem's job as a wellspring of motivation for imaginative undertakings is multi-layered and persevering. From the visual expressions to writing, music, theater, and then some, the city's strict, verifiable, and social aspects have given a wellspring of motivation to craftsmen and masterminds all through the ages.

Jerusalem's impact reaches out past its actual lines, forming worldwide discussions about the crossing points of confidence, culture, and imagination. As a city that spans the heavenly and the natural, the old and the cutting edge, Jerusalem keeps on spellbinding the minds of the individuals who look to investigate the significant and complex embroidery of human experience.

Jerusalem, a city saturated with history and instilled with profound importance, has filled in as a wellspring of motivation for a different exhibit of imaginative undertakings. Its novel situation as a sacrosanct site for Judaism, Christianity, and Islam, combined with its rich verifiable embroidery and social variety, has made it a dream for specialists, scholars, performers, and masterminds across the hundreds of years.

The strict significance of Jerusalem, originating from its relationship with key occasions in the Abrahamic beliefs, is a focal wellspring of motivation. For specialists, the city's strict tourist spots like the Western Wall, the Congregation of the Blessed Tomb, and the Arch of the Stone have given strong visual themes. These hallowed spaces, with their structural glory and verifiable reverberation, have been caught in compositions, figures, and other visual expressions as specialists try to convey the extraordinary and profound elements of Jerusalem.

Essayists, as well, have been attracted to Jerusalem's real's, strict accounts, investigating subjects, personality, and the human experience. The city's importance in the Jewish Book of scriptures, the New Confirmation, and the Quran has propelled abstract works that dig into the intricacies of strict conviction and the transaction between the heavenly and the human. Jerusalem turns into a scholarly person in itself, an image of the everlasting journey for significance and association with the heavenly.

Performers have found motivation in the city's assorted strict customs, making arrangements that mirror the melodic embroidery of Jerusalem. The calls to supplication from minarets, the full hints of place of worship drones, and the psalms sung in temples have all added to a rich melodic legacy. Jerusalem's yearly Oud Celebration, observing Center Eastern music, represents the city's job as a center point for melodic imagination, where craftsmen from various foundations meet up in an agreeable combination of sounds.

Theater, as a type of imaginative articulation, has thrived in Jerusalem, giving a phase to investigating the intricacies of confidence, history, and human connections. The city's auditoriums have facilitated exhibitions that reach from verifiable dramatizations set against the scenery of Jerusalem's past to contemporary plays resolving squeezing social issues. Thanks to theater, specialists dive into the complex idea of Jerusalem's social and verifiable personality, offering crowds a window into the human experience inside the city's walls.

In the domain of writing, Jerusalem has motivated journalists from assorted social and phonetic foundations. Crafted by creators like Amos Oz, Chaim Potok, and Mahmoud Darwish mirror the city's effect on their artistic minds. Whether investigating the interweaving of confidence and governmental issues, the intricacies of personality, or the verifiable layers of the city, these essayists add to a worldwide scholarly discussion formed by the significant impacts of Jerusalem.

The visual expressions, enveloping work of art, mold, and different structures, have been significantly formed by Jerusalem's visual and social scene. The old design, dynamic business sectors, and strict images give a rich range to specialists looking to catch the pith of the city. The juxtaposition of the old and the new, the consecrated and the unremarkable, turns into a wellspring of visual illustration that specialists capably mesh into their works.

Jerusalem's contemporary craftsmanship scene, mirroring a combination of customary and present day impacts, adds a powerful layer to its social commitments. Nearby and worldwide craftsmen take part in a visual exchange that tends to subjects like character, memory, and the effect of international real factors on individual lives. The city's specialty displays and show spaces act as stages for craftsmen to wrestle with Jerusalem's at various times, adding to a more extensive discussion about the convergence of craftsmanship, culture, and society.

Film and visual narrating have tracked down rich ground in Jerusalem, where the city's old and present day components give a convincing scenery to investigating a great many subjects. Narratives and component films shot in Jerusalem frequently act as realistic reflections on the city's intricacies, offering nuanced viewpoints on its social and authentic layers. The visual medium turns into a useful asset for passing the rich embroidery of Jerusalem's stories on to a worldwide crowd.

Music, as an all inclusive language, has been a conductor for communicating the social and strict variety of Jerusalem. The city's yearly Oud Celebration, displaying the gifts of performers from the Center East and then some, is a demonstration of the dynamic melodic customs that meet in Jerusalem. The celebration not just praises the rich legacy of Center Eastern music yet additionally encourages multifaceted coordinated efforts, repeating the city's ethos of agreeable conjunction.

Jerusalem's importance reaches out past the domains of human expressions to scholarly and philosophical talk. The city has been a gathering point for researchers, scholars, and thinkers who take part in exchange on issues of confidence, reason, and the human condition. Jerusalem's effect on the Abrahamic religions has ignited significant reflections on philosophy and reasoning, adding to a worldwide talk that rises above social and strict limits.

Scholarly foundations in Jerusalem, like the Jewish College of Jerusalem and Al-Quds College, act as centers for scholarly pursuits and examination. Researchers from different disciplines merge in the city, investigating subjects going from prehistoric studies and history to writing and philosophy. The scholarly local area in Jerusalem adds to the progression of information, encouraging a feeling of request and decisive reasoning.

Interfaith exchange drives, exemplified by associations like the Elijah Interfaith Foundation, highlight Jerusalem's job as a reference point of strict resistance and understanding. Endeavors to unite researchers, strict pioneers, and masterminds from various confidence customs add to a common investigation of normal qualities and desires. Jerusalem turns into a space for encouraging common regard and collaboration, rising above social and strict contrasts.

Culinary practices in Jerusalem mirror the city's social variety, with flavors and fixings drawn from Jewish, Bedouin, and Christian culinary customs. The clamoring markets, for example, Mahane Yehuda, offer a tangible encounter where the smells of flavors, the shades of new produce, and the hints of merchants join to make a culinary mosaic. Jerusalem's cooking turns into an impression of its multicultural character, a combination of tastes that reflects the city's rich history.

The city's obligation to protecting its social legacy is obvious in rebuilding endeavors that expect to defend its noteworthy destinations and engineering treasures. The Old City, with its old walls and milestones, fills in as a living demonstration of Jerusalem's persevering through heritage. Reclamation projects protect the actual designs as well as add to an aggregate work to guarantee the coherence of Jerusalem's social legacy for people in the future.

Celebrations and occasions in Jerusalem praise the city's social liveliness, giving stages to specialists, performers, and masterminds to feature their abilities. The Jerusalem Celebration of Light, changing the Old City into an enlightened exhibition, features the excellence of its engineering and makes an enchanted air for inhabitants and guests the same. These occasions add to the powerful social embroidery of Jerusalem, encouraging a feeling of local area and shared festival.

All in all, Jerusalem's job as a wellspring of motivation for imaginative undertakings is far reaching and persevering. From the visual expressions to writing, music, theater, and then some, the city's strict, verifiable, and social aspects have given a rich embroidery to specialists and masterminds to draw upon. Jerusalem's impact stretches out a long ways past its actual limits, molding worldwide discussions about the convergences of confidence, culture, and inventiveness. As a city that spans the heavenly and the natural, the old and the cutting edge, Jerusalem keeps on enrapturing the minds of the people who try to investigate the significant and complex embroidery of human experience.

Chapter 4

Jerusalem as a Global Pilgrimage Destination

Jerusalem, the old city that has remained as a demonstration of the combination of history, culture, and confidence, holds a remarkable spot in the hearts of millions all over the planet. As a worldwide journey objective, it entices the dedicated, history specialists, and inquisitive voyagers the same to investigate its holy destinations and unwind the layers of its rich embroidery. The city's importance is well established in the strict customs of Judaism, Christianity, and Islam, making it a point of convergence for otherworldly excursions and social investigation.

For Jews, Jerusalem is the holiest city, respected for its relationship with the Sanctuary Mount and the Western Wall. The Western Wall, otherwise called the Moaning Wall, remains as a leftover of the Subsequent Sanctuary and fills in as a position of supplication and reflection for Jewish travelers. The longing for Jerusalem is implanted in Jewish petitions, customs, and the aggregate memory of a diaspora that has crossed hundreds of years.

In Christianity, Jerusalem possesses a focal job in the existence of Jesus Christ. The Congregation of the Blessed Catacomb, accepted to be the site of Jesus' execution, internment, and revival, draws Christian pioneers from each side of the globe. The Through Dolorosa, the way Jesus is said to have strolled en route to his execution, is set apart by stations of the cross, and travelers follow his means in a grave parade. The meaning of these destinations rises above denominational limits, with Catholics, Conventional Christians, and Protestants figuring out something worth agreeing on in the holiness of Jerusalem.

Islam, as well, holds Jerusalem in high regard. The Vault of the Stone, situated on the Sanctuary Mount, is an image of Islamic design and otherworldliness. The Al-Aqsa Mosque, neighboring the Vault of the Stone, is viewed as the third holiest site in Islam. As per Islamic practice, the Prophet Muhammad was moved from Mecca to Jerusalem during the Night Excursion, underscoring the city's significance to Muslims.

The attractive draw of Jerusalem reaches out past strict limits. Its verifiable importance, formed by an embroidery of developments and domains, is clear in its engineering, roads, and landmarks. The Old City of Jerusalem, an UNESCO World Legacy Site, exemplifies hundreds of years of history inside its walls. Restricted back streets lead to stowed away patios, and the blending fragrances of flavors and incense make a climate that is both ageless and energetic.

The Western Wall, with its endured stones and the requests of the unwavering got into its cleft, remains as a quiet observer to the recurring pattern of history. Travelers approach it with worship, contacting the antiquated stones and emptying their expectations and petitions into the unmistakable history that encompasses them. The Western Wall Square turns into a get-together spot for different articulations of confidence, as Jews from various foundations and sections merge to interface with their legacy.

Christian explorers, bearing crosses and rosaries, navigate the cobblestone roads of the Old City. The Congregation of the Blessed Catacomb, an intricate construction lodging the Golgotha, the Stone of Blessing, and the Edicule encasing the burial chamber of Jesus, turns into a point of convergence of their journey. Each step is an excursion through scriptural stories, and the air is accused of a profound energy that rises above denominational contrasts.

Muslim pioneers, as well, add to the mosaic of Jerusalem's journey story. The Vault of the Stone, with its brilliant arch and complex mosaics, remains as a symbol against the city horizon. The call to petitioning heaven reverberations through the minarets, attracting admirers to the Al-Aqsa Mosque. The esplanade of the Sanctuary Mount turns into a space where the profound and the verifiable join, welcoming Muslims to interface with the holy tradition of their confidence.

The interlacing of these strict stories makes a mind boggling and agreeable embroidery that characterizes Jerusalem as a worldwide journey objective. The city's status as a blessed site for various beliefs has, on occasion, been a wellspring of strain and struggle.

The contending cases to the Sanctuary Mount, the blessed site for the two Jews and Muslims, have ignited political and strict questions that reverberation through the ages.

The international scene of Jerusalem is all around as multifaceted as its strict embroidered artwork. The city has been vanquished and reconquered by various realms, including the Babylonians, Persians, Greeks, Romans, Byzantines, Bedouins, Crusaders, Ottomans, and English. Every hero influenced the city, molding its engineering, culture, and character. The assorted impacts are noticeable in the shifted design styles that exist together inside the city walls.

The Crusader engineering, exemplified by structures like the Congregation of the Blessed Tomb, mirrors the archaic European presence in the Heavenly Land. The Ottoman impact is obvious in structures like the Pinnacle of David, a stronghold that has filled different needs over the entire course of time. The English Order, which followed the breakdown of the Ottoman Domain after The Second Great War, transformed the city's managerial and metropolitan design.

The Old City itself is separated into four quarters — Jewish, Christian, Muslim, and Armenian — each with its own unmistakable person and tourist spots. The clamoring markets of the Muslim Quarter, the peaceful yards of the Christian Quarter, the tight rear entryways of the Jewish Quarter, and the Armenian Quarter's old places of worship make a kaleidoscope of encounters inside the old walls.

In spite of the international difficulties and strict strains, Jerusalem keeps on being a signal for pioneers looking for a more profound association with their confidence and history. The city's versatility, clear in its capacity to endure hundreds of years of contention and change, adds a layer of otherworldly importance to the journey insight. Pioneers frequently get themselves not just backtracking the means of prophets and holy people yet in addition exploring the intricacies of a city that is both old and current, sacrosanct and challenged.

The journey to Jerusalem isn't only an actual excursion; a profound odyssey rises above reality. Pioneers show up with a feeling of expectation, conveying with them the heaviness of hundreds of years of custom and the narratives of the people who preceded. The demonstration of journey turns into a method for interfacing with a bigger story, one that stretches back to the starting points of their confidence.

The excursion to Jerusalem is much of the time a groundbreaking encounter, a journey of the spirit. Travelers, whether they come as people or as a component of coordinated gatherings, set out on a journey for profound reestablishment and edification. The holy locales become waypoints in this excursion, offering snapshots of reflection, supplication, and fellowship with the heavenly. The stones of Jerusalem, endured by time and history, become conductors for the transmission of confidence across ages.

The ceremonies related with journey in Jerusalem are basically as different as the strict customs that merge in the city. For Jews, the journey toward the Western Wall includes the arrangement of composed petitions in the hole of the antiquated stones. The musical influencing of the body while discussing petitions to heaven makes a feeling of closeness with the heavenly presence accepted to live in the leftovers of the Subsequent Sanctuary.

Christian pioneers participate in a bunch of customs, from remembering the means of Jesus along the Through Dolorosa to partaking in the Blessed Fire function at the Congregation of the Sacred Mausoleum. The Stone of Blessing, where Jesus' body is said to have been arranged for entombment, turns into a point of convergence for custom blessing and supplication. Explorers from various Christian groups meet up in shared worship for the holy locales.

Muslim explorers, as well, participate in ceremonies that interface them to the otherworldly tradition of Jerusalem. The circumambulation of the Vault of the Stone, the exhibition of supplications in the Al-Aqsa Mosque, and the aggregate Friday petitions on the Sanctuary Mount add to the hallowed air of the city. Travelers frequently carry with them the accounts of the Prophet's Night Process, reconsidering the divine journey that is said to have occurred from Mecca to Jerusalem.

The union of these ceremonies makes an unmistakable feeling of the sacrosanct in Jerusalem. Pioneers travel through the city with a love that rises above strict limits, perceiving the common sacredness of the destinations they visit. The demonstration of journey turns into an extension between the individual and the group, a string that interfaces the present to the past and what's in store.

Jerusalem's job as a worldwide journey objective reaches out past the strict circle. The city is a living exhibition hall, a store of relics and verifiable fortunes that give testimony regarding the unfurling show of human development. The Israel Historical center, situated in Jerusalem, houses a different assortment that traverses the centuries, including the Dead Ocean Parchments, old relics, and current Israeli workmanship.

The Pinnacle of David Gallery, arranged inside the old fortification, offers an excursion through Jerusalem's set of experiences, from its earliest days to the present. Shows follow the city's advancement under various rulers and investigate the subjects of religion, culture, and concurrence. The actual gallery is a demonstration of the layers of history that have formed Jerusalem, with its Crusader, Mamluk, and Ottoman design.

Jerusalem's status as a journey objective is likewise connected to its scholarly and imaginative legacy. The city has been a dream for writers, journalists, and craftsmen all through the ages. Crafted by William Blake, T.S. Eliot, and Yehuda Amichai mirror the profound and existential elements of Jerusalem. The city's assorted scenes, from the Mount of Olives to the Kidron Valley, have propelled painters and photographic artists to catch its substance in clear detail.

Past its strict and verifiable importance, Jerusalem is a microcosm of the intricacies of conjunction. The city's different populace, including Jews, Christians, Muslims, and Armenians, mirrors an embroidery of societies and customs. The interlacing of these networks inside the walls of the Old City is a demonstration of the chance of tranquil concurrence in the midst of the difficulties of history and governmental issues.

Notwithstanding, the truth of Jerusalem is set apart by the continuous Israeli-Palestinian struggle, which has significant ramifications for the city's status and the elements of journey. The political and regional questions encompassing East Jerusalem, caught by Israel during the 1967 Six-Day War, have escalated strains and molded the journey insight. The challenged idea of the city adds a layer of intricacy to the demonstration of journey, as guests explore the political real factors that converge with their profound excursion.

The subject of admittance to heavenly destinations turns into a point of convergence in the political talk encompassing Jerusalem. The situation with the Sanctuary Mount/Haram al-Sharif is an especially delicate issue, with contending cases and limitations on access filling strict and political strains. The continuous discussions over the acknowledgment of Jerusalem as the capital of Israel, the migration of unfamiliar consulates to the city, and the development of Israeli settlements in East Jerusalem further confound the journey scene.

In this specific circumstance, journey to Jerusalem turns into a demonstration of declaration, an assertion of the getting through otherworldly and verifiable association with the city. Explorers, no matter what their strict alliance, explore the international real factors with an assurance to interface with the sacrosanct destinations that hold significant importance for their confidence. The demonstration of journey, notwithstanding political difficulties, turns into a type of opposition and flexibility, a reaffirmation of the persevering through significance of Jerusalem in the hearts of devotees.

The effect of innovation on the journey insight in Jerusalem is a subject of continuous investigation. The appearance of mass the travel industry, mechanical headways, and changes in international scenes have changed the elements of journey. Explorers, when restricted by the difficulties of movement and correspondence, presently approach an abundance of data and assets that shape their assumptions and cooperations with the hallowed destinations.

The advanced age has additionally brought about virtual journeys, permitting people to remotely encounter the holy destinations of Jerusalem. Virtual visits, online gatherings, and live-streamed strict services give a virtual association with the city for the individuals who might confront physical, monetary, or political hindrances to journey. While these advanced encounters can never completely imitate the tactile wealth of being truly present in Jerusalem, they open up additional opportunities for commitment with the consecrated.

The commodification of journey is one more part of innovation that has impacted the journey insight. The development of the travel industry in Jerusalem has prompted the improvement of foundation, administrations, and business ventures taking care of the requirements of pioneers. Journey has become a profound excursion as well as an attractive item, with visit bundles, manuals, and strict memorabilia adding to the monetary scene of the city.

The commercialization of journey brings up moral issues about the harmony between otherworldly realness and business interests. The test lies in saving the holiness of the journey insight while recognizing the monetary real factors that support the city and its hallowed destinations. Finding some kind of harmony is significant to guarantee that journey stays a groundbreaking and significant excursion as opposed to a simple exchange.

All in all, Jerusalem's status as a worldwide journey objective is a real demonstration of the getting through force, history, and culture. The city's consecrated destinations, formed by the accounts of Judaism, Christianity, and Islam, draw explorers from different foundations and convictions. The journey insight in Jerusalem is a multi-layered venture, enveloping otherworldly, verifiable, and social aspects.

Notwithstanding the difficulties presented by international relations, the commercialization of journey, and the intricacies of conjunction, Jerusalem keeps on being an attractive community for those looking for a more profound association with their confidence and legacy. The city's flexibility, reflected in its old stones and energetic networks, adds a layer of importance to the demonstration of journey. Whether drew nearer as an actual excursion or a virtual investigation, the journey to Jerusalem stays an immortal mission for significance, a quest for the holy in the core of an old city that keeps on moving wonder and respect.

4.1 Investigating the phenomenon of pilgrimage to Jerusalem from different parts of the world.

The peculiarity of journey to Jerusalem is an intricate and complex articulation of human otherworldliness, social personality, and verifiable association. Individuals from various regions of the planet set out on excursions to this old city, drawn by the strict importance, verifiable reverberation, and the commitment of a groundbreaking encounter. Researching the inspirations, customs, and effects of journey to Jerusalem offers a nuanced comprehension of the manners by which this worldwide journey peculiarity shapes individual and aggregate characters.

One of the focal inspirations for journey to Jerusalem lies in its strict importance. The city holds a worshipped spot in the three significant monotheistic religions — Judaism, Christianity, and Islam. For Jews, Jerusalem is the everlasting capital and the holiest city, key to their strict practices and aggregate memory. The Western Wall, a remainder of the

Subsequent Sanctuary, fills in as a point of convergence for Jewish supplication and journey, representing an association with a verifiable and profound heritage.

For Christians, Jerusalem is complicatedly connected to the life and lessons of Jesus Christ. The Congregation of the Blessed Mausoleum, accepted to envelop the destinations of Jesus' execution, entombment, and revival, attracts Christian pioneers looking to develop their confidence and experience the substantial association with scriptural occasions. The By means of Dolorosa, the way Jesus is said to have strolled while heading to the execution, turns into a hallowed course for explorers remembering his means and pondering the meaning of their excursion.

In Islam, Jerusalem is regarded as the third holiest city, and the Vault of the Stone stands as an engineering wonder on the Sanctuary Mount. The Al-Aqsa Mosque, adjoining the Arch of the Stone, holds significant importance in Islamic custom, especially as the site from which the Prophet Muhammad is accepted to have rose to the sky during the Night Excursion. Muslim explorers meet on Jerusalem to participate in petitions, circumambulation, and aggregate love on the esplanade of the Sanctuary Mount.

The strict inspirations for journey to Jerusalem are not restricted to these three significant Abrahamic beliefs. The city is additionally huge for other strict customs, and individuals from assorted profound foundations are attracted to its sacrosanct destinations. The peculiarity of journey hence turns into a worldwide embroidery woven with strings of strict variety, mirroring a common love for Jerusalem's profound legacy.

Past strict inspirations, journey to Jerusalem is many times driven by a longing for verifiable association and social investigation. The city's antiquated walls encase layers of history traversing centuries. The Old City, with its limited rear entryways and notable milestones, turns into a living gallery that welcomes travelers to step back in time. The Western Wall, the Congregation of the Heavenly Catacomb, and the Arch of the Stone are strict locales as well as living observers to the ascent and fall of domains, the battles of civilizations, and the persevering through human journey for importance.

The Pinnacle of David, a fortress inside the Old City, fills in as a historical center chronicling Jerusalem's set of experiences. Travelers investigate shows that follow the city's advancement through the ages, from the hour of the Canaanites and Jebusites to its triumph by David and the development of the Main Sanctuary. The Crusader, Mamluk, and Ottoman periods are strikingly depicted, featuring the assorted impacts that have formed Jerusalem's engineering and social scene.

Journey to Jerusalem is, in this manner, a strict excursion as well as a verifiable and social odyssey. Pioneers, as they cross the cobblestone roads and old designs, draw in with the unmistakable leftovers of a former time. The effect of history on the journey experience is substantial, making a feeling of association with the stories that have unfurled inside the city's walls.

The international setting of Jerusalem further adds layers of intricacy to the peculiarity of journey. The city has been a point of convergence of political and strict strains for quite a long time, and the unsettled Israeli-Palestinian struggle keeps on molding the journey scene. The situation with East Jerusalem, caught by Israel during the 1967 Six-Day War, stays a disputed matter, with contending cases and global debates impacting admittance to blessed locales.

The Sanctuary Mount/Haram al-Sharif, specifically, is a flashpoint for political and strict contentions. The contending cases of Jews and Muslims to this hallowed space have prompted limitations, periodic savagery, and a sensitive overall influence. Travelers explore the strict meaning of the destinations as well as the international real factors that cross with their otherworldly excursion. The demonstration of journey becomes weaved with the more extensive story of political battles, regional debates, and the mission for concurrence in a separated city.

The effect of the international setting isn't just felt in the actual space of Jerusalem yet additionally in the accounts and talks encompassing journey. Explorers frequently wrestle with inquiries of equity, common freedoms, and the moral components of their excursion. The choice to embrace a journey to Jerusalem turns into an assertion on one's position toward the complex political real factors of the district, and travelers might end up drawing in with issues of civil rights and peacebuilding as vital parts of their otherworldly excursion.

Innovation has acquainted new aspects with the peculiarity of journey to Jerusalem. The approach of mass transportation, data innovation, and globalization has worked with the development of explorers from various corners of the world. Journey, when a difficult and burdensome endeavor, has become more open to a bigger number of individuals, rising above geological limits and social obstructions.

The computerized age has additionally led to virtual journeys, permitting people to draw in with the sacrosanct destinations of Jerusalem without truly being available. Virtual visits, live-streamed strict functions, and online gatherings make a computerized space for pioneers to associate, share encounters, and take part in the aggregate journey story. While virtual journeys can't completely imitate the tangible and exemplified insight of being nearby, they offer an interesting type of commitment for the individuals who might confront physical, monetary, or political limitations.

The commodification of journey is one more part of advancement that impacts the peculiarity. The development of the travel industry in Jerusalem has prompted the improvement of framework, administrations, and business endeavors taking care of the necessities of explorers. Journey has turned into an attractive item, with visit bundles, manuals, and strict memorabilia adding to the monetary scene of the city.

The commercialization of journey brings up moral issues about the harmony between otherworldly realness and business interests. Pioneers should explore the strain between the commodified parts of their excursion and the mission for a certifiable and groundbreaking experience. Finding some kind of harmony is vital to guarantee that journey stays a significant and legitimate articulation of confidence, instead of a consumerist exchange.

The effect of journey on the host local area is a significant aspect that merits consideration in the examination of this peculiarity. Jerusalem, as a worldwide journey objective, isn't just an otherworldly focus yet additionally a social and financial center point. The inundation of pioneers adds to the neighborhood economy, supporting organizations, lodgings, and the travel industry area. Notwithstanding, it likewise presents difficulties connected with foundation, natural supportability, and the protection of social legacy.

The conjunction of various strict and social networks inside Jerusalem adds one more layer to the effect of journey. The Old City, with its unmistakable quarters — Jewish, Christian, Muslim, and Armenian — represents the intertwining of different networks. The elements of living next to each other in a space of significant strict importance require progressing exchange, understanding, and a pledge to tranquil concurrence.

The examination of journey to Jerusalem should likewise consider the mental and individual elements of the journey insight. Pioneers frequently depict their excursion as a groundbreaking and thoughtful cycle. The actual demonstration of making a trip to Jerusalem, drawing in with consecrated locales, and taking part in customs makes a space for reflection, consideration, and otherworldly development.

The aggregate idea of journey encourages a feeling of local area and common perspective among explorers. The experiences with individuals from various foundations, societies, and convictions add to a more extensive comprehension of mankind and the interconnectedness of confidence customs. Travelers frequently get back from their excursions with a recharged feeling of direction, a developed profound association, and a promise to encouraging comprehension and harmony.

4.2 Discussing the economic and cultural impact of pilgrimages on the city.

Journeys to Jerusalem, well established in strict customs and verifiable stories, reach out past their otherworldly importance to socially affect the city. The union of pioneers from assorted foundations adds to Jerusalem's monetary energy, supporting organizations, inns, and the travel industry area. At the same time, the social elements of the city are improved as it turns into a mixture of customs, cultivating a one of a kind environment of conjunction and trade.

The monetary effect of journeys on Jerusalem is clear in the clamoring exercises that go with the convergence of explorers. The travel industry, firmly connected with journey, fills in as a significant financial driver for the city. Travelers, whether showing up exclusively or in co-ordinated gatherings, add to the nearby economy by belittling lodgings, eateries, transportation administrations, and keepsake shops. The interest for facilities during top journey seasons animates the cordiality area, giving work and pay to nearby organizations.

Jerusalem's Old City, with its tangled roads and dynamic business sectors, turns into a point of convergence for monetary exercises driven by journeys. The different quarters — Jewish, Christian, Muslim, and Armenian — house a heap of organizations taking special care of the necessities and inclinations of pioneers. From customary business sectors offering strict relics and social memorabilia to present day foundations offering various administrations, the financial scene of the Old City is molded by the recurring pattern of traveler traffic.

The Western Wall Square, a critical site for Jewish explorers, changes into a mutual space where admirers accumulate for petition and reflection. Encompassing regions see a flood in monetary movement as shops and merchants take care of the requirements of the unwavering. Likewise, the area of the Congregation of the Heavenly Catacomb turns into a clamoring commercial center, offering strict things, trinkets, and rewards to Christian pioneers and guests.

The financial effect isn't restricted to the quick area of strict destinations; it swells through the whole city. Pioneers frequently take part in long-term visits, investigating the hallowed destinations as well as the more extensive social and verifiable contributions of Jerusalem. Historical centers, displays, and social establishments benefit from expanded footfall, adding to the city's in general financial wellbeing.

The supportability of Jerusalem's economy is intently attached to its capacity to adjust the advantages of journey related exercises with the conservation of its social and verifiable legacy. While traveler driven the travel industry is a critical wellspring of income, it likewise presents difficulties connected with framework, ecological manageability, and the safeguarding of the city's interesting person. Finding some kind of harmony between financial development and social protection is fundamental to guarantee the drawn out prosperity of the city.

Notwithstanding its monetary effect, journey to Jerusalem shapes the social scene of the city, encouraging a climate of social trade, understanding, and conjunction. Jerusalem, with its rich history and various networks, turns into a gathering point for individuals from various regions of the planet, each carrying their exceptional social viewpoints to the city.

The Old City's quarters, each related with a specific strict practice, act as spaces where various societies meet. Pioneers, as they travel through the thin roads and collaborate with the nearby populace, become piece of a unique social trade.

The Old City's business sectors, loaded up with the fragrances of flavors, the hints of different dialects, and seeing conventional pieces of clothing, embody the combination of societies that happens during journey seasons.

The social effect of journeys isn't restricted to the Old City. Exhibition halls and social foundations in Jerusalem assume an essential part in teaching explorers about the city's set of experiences, strict importance, and social legacy. The Israel Historical center, for instance, houses relics from different periods, offering explorers a more extensive comprehension of the intricate embroidery that makes up Jerusalem's social personality.

Pioneers, thusly, add to the social imperativeness of Jerusalem by drawing in with nearby customs and taking part in widespread developments. The city turns into a phase for strict services, parades, and customs that grandstand the variety of confidence customs. These occasions improve the social texture of Jerusalem as well as give open doors to interfaith exchange and understanding.

The joining of various social impacts in Jerusalem makes an exceptional air of concurrence. The city's different populace, including Jews, Christians, Muslims, and Armenians, mirrors a mosaic of social customs. Journeys add to this variety by presenting new points of view, cultivating a feeling of receptiveness, and empowering discourse among individuals of various foundations.

The effect of social trade isn't restricted to the span of journeys; it reaches out to the more extensive local area. Nearby organizations, affected by the inclinations and tastes of pioneers, may integrate components of assorted societies into their contributions. Cafés, for instance, may present dishes roused by the culinary practices of travelers' nations of origin. This diverse trade upgrades the city's social energy as well as encourages a feeling of shared regard and understanding.

In any case, the social effect of journeys isn't without its difficulties. The deluge of guests, while advancing the social woven artwork, likewise represents the gamble of social commodification. Customary practices and curios might be decreased to simple wares available to be purchased, weakening their credible social importance. Adjusting the longing for social trade with the requirement for aware and manageable commitment is fundamental to guarantee that the effect of journeys on Jerusalem's way of life is positive and persevering.

The job of journey in encouraging interfaith exchange and understanding is a urgent part of its social effect. Jerusalem, as a city hallowed to numerous beliefs, turns into a characteristic space for experiences between individuals of various strict customs. Travelers, directed by a typical love for the city's strict destinations, frequently find potential open doors for significant cooperations that rise above strict limits.

Interfaith discourse turns out to be especially apparent in shared spaces inside the Old City. The Western Wall Court, for example, is a social occasion point for Jews from different sections, each coming the holy site with their particular ceremonies and customs. The

Congregation of the Heavenly Catacomb comparatively obliges different Christian categories, encouraging a feeling of collaboration and shared worship for the site.

The interfaith dynamic likewise reaches out to drives and occasions coordinated by nearby networks and strict organizations. Interfaith petitioning heaven administrations, addresses, and comprehensive developments give stages to discourse, advancing common regard and understanding among explorers of various beliefs. These drives add to the development of an ethos of resilience and concurrence in Jerusalem.

Regardless of the positive social effects, journey to Jerusalem additionally can possibly enhance existing pressures and add to social misconceptions. The covering cases to heavenly destinations, especially in the challenged region of the Old City, may prompt contentions among various strict networks. Aversion to social subtleties, regard for neighborhood customs, and a promise to serene concurrence are essential in moderating possible difficulties and guaranteeing that the effect of journeys is a power for social enhancement.

4.3 Exploring the experiences of pilgrims and their role in shaping the global perception of Jerusalem.

The encounters of explorers in Jerusalem are significant and multi-layered, forming individual profound excursions as well as adding to the more extensive worldwide view of the city. Pioneers, driven by strict commitment and a journey for importance, draw in with Jerusalem's holy destinations, various societies, and complex history in manners that rise above geological and social limits. Understanding the encounters of pioneers gives bits of knowledge into the groundbreaking force of journey and its effect on forming an aggregate story about Jerusalem.

At the core of the explorer experience in Jerusalem is the commitment with hallowed destinations that hold significant strict importance. For Jewish pioneers, the Western Wall remains as a substantial association with the remainders of the Subsequent Sanctuary. The demonstration of moving toward the old stones, contacting them, and putting composed petitions inside the cleft turns into a profoundly private and shared articulation of commitment. The Western Wall Square, where Jews from different foundations combine for supplication, makes a feeling of solidarity in variety, as people from various sections meet up in a common veneration for their consecrated legacy.

Christian travelers, then again, track down their profound point of convergence in the Congregation of the Blessed Mausoleum. The excursion through the By means of Dolorosa, remembering the means of Jesus while heading to the execution, turns into a strong custom of reflection and recognizable proof with the enduring of Christ.

The Stone of Blessing, where Jesus' body is said to have been arranged for internment, turns into a position of personal supplication and blessing for Christian travelers. The vivid experience inside the Congregation of the Blessed Mausoleum, with its rich imagery and verifiable layers, adds to an extended comprehension of the Christian confidence.

Muslim travelers, as well, draw in with the holy locales of Jerusalem, especially the Vault of the Stone and the Al-Aqsa Mosque on the Sanctuary Mount. The esplanade of the Sanctuary Mount turns into a space for aggregate supplications, consideration, and the circumambulation of the Vault of the Stone. The tangible encounters of the call to supplication, the unpredictable engineering, and the all encompassing perspectives on the city add to a profound excursion that interfaces Muslims to the verifiable and strict tradition of Jerusalem.

These singular strict encounters combine in the common spaces of the Old City, making a rich embroidery of social and otherworldly variety. Explorers, wearing clothing intelligent of their confidence customs, explore the restricted roads, take part in ceremonies, and take an interest in the day to day existence of the city. The intermixing of different societies inside the Old City turns into a microcosm of the worldwide strict mosaic, encouraging a feeling of interconnectedness among pioneers from various corners of the world.

The extraordinary idea of journey is clear in the stories of individual explorers. Many depict their encounters in Jerusalem as life changing, described by snapshots of significant otherworldly understanding, self-revelation, and an elevated familiarity with the interconnectedness of humankind. The demonstration of journey turns into a journey of the spirit, an excursion internal that reflects the outer investigation of sacrosanct spaces.

The extraordinary effect isn't restricted to the span of the journey; it stretches out into the explorers' lives upon their get back. Travelers frequently convey with them a recharged feeling of direction, a developed obligation to their confidence, and an increased aversion to civil rights issues. The encounters of journey shape individual ways of life as well as add to the worldwide impression of Jerusalem as a city that has the ability to rouse, change, and interface individuals across strict and social partitions.

The worldwide view of Jerusalem, impacted by the encounters of pioneers, is a complicated exchange of strict, social, and verifiable stories. The city's status as a heavenly site for Judaism, Christianity, and Islam positions it as a point of convergence for the common legacy of monotheistic beliefs. Explorers, through their stories and declarations, add to the development of an aggregate picture of Jerusalem that rises above the international difficulties and strict pressures that frequently overwhelm the titles.

The job of explorers in molding the worldwide impression of Jerusalem is enhanced by their job as social representatives. As explorers return to their networks, they convey with them strict bits of knowledge as well as a social comprehension of Jerusalem.

The different social trades that happen inside the Old City, the commitment with nearby customs, and the seeing of interfaith elements become stories that, when shared, add to a more nuanced and refined depiction of Jerusalem on the worldwide stage.

The effect of travelers as social representatives is especially obvious in the time of advanced availability. Travelers, furnished with cell phones and web-based entertainment, record their encounters continuously, sharing pictures, recordings, and reflections with a worldwide crowd.

Virtual journeys, worked with by innovation, permit individuals all over the planet to vicariously draw in with the sacrosanct destinations of Jerusalem and take part in the aggregate story of journey. Web-based entertainment stages become channels for the scattering of different social and strict viewpoints, molding a more comprehensive and diverse worldwide impression of the city.

Nonetheless, the job of pioneers in molding the worldwide view of Jerusalem isn't without challenges. The potential for social allotment, distortion, and misrepresentation of mind boggling strict and verifiable accounts exists, particularly in the time of online entertainment where data spreads quickly. Pioneers, as social representatives, bear an obligation to convey the lavishness and intricacy of Jerusalem's character, keeping away from reductionist or cliché depictions that might add to false impressions.

The international setting of Jerusalem, set apart by the Israeli-Palestinian struggle and contending cases to heavenly locales, adds a layer of intricacy to the worldwide insight formed by pioneers. Explorers might end up exploring political awarenesses, drawing in with inquiries of equity, and battling with the more extensive accounts of the area. The effect of journey on the worldwide impression of Jerusalem, hence, happens inside a system that is both strictly huge and politically charged.

Journey, as a peculiarity that rises above individual encounters to shape an aggregate story, adds to the talk on the meaning of Jerusalem in worldwide cognizance. The city, with its layers of history, social variety, and strict significance, turns into a point of convergence for conversations on interfaith relations, social trade, and the common legacy of humankind. Pioneers, through their collaborations, stories, and computerized commitment, become specialists in forming a worldwide discernment that goes past the titles and political discussions.

The aggregate story developed by travelers likewise assumes a part in impacting global talk and strategies connected with Jerusalem. The voices of the individuals who have encountered the city firsthand convey a weight that reaches out past strict or social affiliations. Pioneers, by sharing their accounts and viewpoints, add to a more thorough comprehension of Jerusalem that envelops its strict, verifiable, and social aspects. This, thus, may impact popular assessment, scholarly conversations, and strategic contemplations connected with the city's status and future.

All in all, investigating the encounters of travelers in Jerusalem uncovers a unique exchange between individual profound excursions and the more extensive worldwide impression of the city. Explorers, driven by strict commitment and a journey for importance, draw in with consecrated locales, explore different societies, and add to the social embroidery of the Old City. Their extraordinary encounters, recorded and partook in the computerized age, become stories that shape the worldwide impression of Jerusalem as a city that rises above strict and social partitions. The job of explorers as social envoys and specialists of an aggregate story highlights the significant effect of journey on the way the world sees and grasps this old and sacrosanct city.

The job of pioneers in molding the worldwide view of Jerusalem is a multi-layered and significant peculiarity that reaches out past individual strict encounters. Pioneers, by ethicalness of their profound excursions, add to the development of an aggregate story about Jerusalem, impacting how the city is seen on a worldwide scale. This impact is especially articulated in the transaction between private accounts, social trades, and the more extensive international setting that characterizes the city.

At the center of the pioneer experience is the profound commitment with consecrated locales that hold critical strict significance. For Jewish explorers, the Western Wall fills in as a strong connection to the remainders of the Subsequent Sanctuary and turns into a space for public petition and reflection. The demonstration of setting composed supplications inside the fissure of the old stones represents an unmistakable association with a verifiable and profound inheritance. The Western Wall Square, where various Jewish categories accumulate, highlights a common veneration that rises above strict contrasts, adding to a feeling of solidarity inside the Jewish confidence.

Christian explorers, then again, center their otherworldly excursion around the Congregation of the Sacred Catacomb. The Through Dolorosa, the way accepted to have been strolled by Jesus while heading to his execution, turns into a journey course of significant importance. Explorers take part in ceremonies of reflection and ID with the enduring of Christ, coming full circle in the vivid experience inside the Congregation of the Heavenly Mausoleum itself. The Stone of Blessing, related with the planning of Jesus' body for entombment, turns into a site of individual and public importance, extending the Christian pioneer's association with the primary occasions of their confidence.

Muslim pioneers, as well, find profound reverberation in the consecrated locales of Jerusalem, especially the Arch of the Stone and the Al-Aqsa Mosque on the Sanctuary Mount. The esplanade of the Sanctuary Mount turns into a space for aggregate supplications, circumambulation, and consideration.

The call to supplication, the unpredictable engineering, and the all encompassing perspectives on the city add to a profound excursion that interfaces Muslims to the verifiable and strict tradition of Jerusalem. The common worship for these locales cultivates a feeling of solidarity among Muslim explorers, no matter what their different social foundations.

These singular strict encounters unite inside the Old City, making a rich embroidery of social and otherworldly variety. Pioneers, wearing clothing intelligent of their confidence customs, explore the thin roads, participate in ceremonies, and partake in the day to day routine of the city. The blending of assorted societies inside the Old City turns into a microcosm of the worldwide strict mosaic, cultivating a feeling of interconnectedness among pioneers from various corners of the world.

The groundbreaking idea of journey is a repetitive subject in the stories of individual pioneers. Many portray their encounters in Jerusalem as life changing, described by snapshots of significant profound knowledge, self-revelation, and an elevated familiarity with the interconnectedness of humankind. The demonstration of journey turns into a journey of the spirit, an excursion internal that reflects the outside investigation of consecrated spaces.

The extraordinary effect isn't bound to the term of the journey; it reaches out into the explorers' lives upon their get back. Travelers frequently convey with them a reestablished feeling of direction, a developed obligation to their confidence, and an elevated aversion to civil rights issues. The encounters of journey shape individual ways of life as well as add to the worldwide impression of Jerusalem as a city that has the ability to motivate, change, and interface individuals across strict and social partitions.

The worldwide impression of Jerusalem, impacted by the encounters of travelers, is a complicated exchange of strict, social, and verifiable stories. The city's status as a heavenly site for Judaism, Christianity, and Islam positions it as a point of convergence for the common legacy of monotheistic beliefs. Travelers, through their stories and declarations, add to the development of an aggregate picture of Jerusalem that rises above the international difficulties and strict strains that frequently rule the titles.

The job of travelers in forming the worldwide view of Jerusalem is enhanced by their job as social representatives. As travelers return to their networks, they convey with them strict experiences as well as a social comprehension of Jerusalem. The different social trades that happen inside the Old City, the commitment with neighborhood customs, and the seeing of interfaith elements become stories that, when shared, add to a more nuanced and refined depiction of Jerusalem on the worldwide stage.

The effect of pioneers as social diplomats is especially obvious in the period of advanced availability. Pioneers, outfitted with cell phones and web-based entertainment, report their encounters continuously, sharing pictures, recordings, and reflections with a worldwide crowd.

Virtual journeys, worked with by innovation, permit individuals all over the planet to vicariously draw in with the consecrated locales of Jerusalem and partake in the aggregate account of journey. Web-based entertainment stages become channels for the dispersal of different social and strict points of view, molding a more comprehensive and diverse worldwide impression of the city.

Nonetheless, the job of pioneers in forming the worldwide impression of Jerusalem isn't without challenges. The potential for social appointment, distortion, and misrepresentation of complicated strict and authentic accounts exists, particularly in the period of virtual entertainment where data spreads quickly. Travelers, as social envoys, bear an obligation to convey the lavishness and intricacy of Jerusalem's personality, staying away from reductionist or cliché depictions that might add to errors.

The international setting of Jerusalem, set apart by the Israeli-Palestinian clash and contending cases to sacred locales, adds a layer of intricacy to the worldwide insight formed by pioneers. Travelers might wind up exploring political responsive qualities, drawing in with inquiries of equity, and battling with the more extensive stories of the locale. The effect of journey on the worldwide impression of Jerusalem, in this way, happens inside a structure that is both strictly huge and politically charged.

Journey, as a peculiarity that rises above individual encounters to shape an aggregate story, adds to the talk on the meaning of Jerusalem in worldwide cognizance. The city, with its layers of history, social variety, and strict significance, turns into a point of convergence for conversations on interfaith relations, social trade, and the common legacy of humankind. Pioneers, through their cooperations, stories, and computerized commitment, become specialists in molding a worldwide discernment that goes past the titles and political discussions.

The aggregate story developed by explorers likewise assumes a part in impacting worldwide talk and strategies connected with Jerusalem. The voices of the people who have encountered the city firsthand convey a weight that reaches out past strict or social affiliations. Travelers, by sharing their accounts and viewpoints, add to a more thorough comprehension of Jerusalem that envelops its strict, verifiable, and social aspects. This, thusly, may impact general assessment, scholastic conversations, and conciliatory contemplations connected with the city's status and future.

Investigating the encounters of pioneers in Jerusalem uncovers a powerful transaction between individual profound excursions and the more extensive worldwide view of the city. Explorers, driven by strict commitment and a mission for significance, draw in with consecrated destinations, explore different societies, and add to the social embroidery of the Old City.

Their groundbreaking encounters, recorded and partook in the computerized age, become stories that shape the worldwide impression of Jerusalem as a city that rises above strict and social partitions. The job of travelers as social ministers and specialists of an aggregate story highlights the significant effect of journey on the way the world sees and grasps this old and holy city.

5

Chapter 5

Interfaith Dialogue and Peace Initiatives

Interfaith exchange and harmony drives stand as critical parts in the worldwide quest for amicability and conjunction among different strict networks. In a world set apart by social pluralism and strict variety, encouraging comprehension and joint effort among various confidence customs becomes basic for the advancement of resilience, shared regard, and serene dwelling together. This talk means to investigate the meaning of interfaith exchange and harmony drives, their verifiable setting, challenges they face, and the potential they hold in tending to contemporary contentions and advancing a more brought together world.

The underlying foundations of interfaith discourse can be followed back to different authentic periods and areas where various strict networks cooperated. From the beginning of time, experiences between various confidence customs have frequently prompted struggle, however they have likewise filled in as any open doors for exchange and shared understanding. The Silk Street, for example, worked with social and strict trades among East and West, encouraging a climate where different conviction frameworks could coincide and gain from one another.

Likewise, the middle age Islamic caliphates saw a thriving of scholarly trade among Muslim, Christian, and Jewish researchers in Spain, known as the Convivencia, featuring a verifiable point of reference for strict conjunction.

In the contemporary period, the requirement for interfaith exchange has become more articulated as globalization, relocation, and mechanical advances interface individuals across beforehand outlandish limits. Strict variety is currently a principal trait of numerous social orders, and the difficulties of strict pluralism require deliberate endeavors to advance comprehension and cooperation among various confidence networks. Interfaith exchange, thusly, arises as a device to connect the holes between different strict practices, cultivating a feeling of shared mankind and normal qualities.

At the core of interfaith exchange is the acknowledgment of the inborn pride and worth of every person, no matter what their strict connection. It looks to fabricate spans between networks, rising above social and strict contrasts to figure out something worth agreeing on. Through open and conscious correspondence, followers of various beliefs can investigate their common qualities, moral standards, and shared objectives. This cycle not just works with a more profound comprehension of one another's convictions yet in addition scatters generalizations and misinterpretations that might add to pressure and struggle.

Interfaith exchange includes a scope of exercises, from casual conversations and instructive projects to formal gatherings and cooperative undertakings. Interfaith drives frequently include strict pioneers, researchers, and experts participating in significant discussions to investigate religious likenesses, moral lessons, and the potential for joint endeavors in tending to shared difficulties. The objective isn't to homogenize strict customs however to see the value in their variety while perceiving the shared conviction that can act as an establishment for participation.

One huge part of interfaith discourse is its commitment to compromise and peacebuilding. Many contentions all over the planet have well established strict aspects, and resolving these issues requires a nuanced comprehension of the different strict scenes included. Interfaith harmony drives try to unite strict pioneers and networks to pursue shared objectives, for example, advancing civil rights, mitigating destitution, and upholding for common freedoms. By utilizing the ethical power of strict pioneers and the shared strength of strict networks, these drives can assume a significant part in encouraging compromise and forestalling further savagery.

At times, interfaith exchange has been instrumental in intervening struggles and working with nonaggression treaties. The Sant'Egidio People group, a Catholic lay affiliation, assumed an essential part in facilitating the nonaggression treaty that finished the Mozambican Nationwide conflict in 1992. The people group participated in discourse with heads of the fighting gatherings, stressing shared values and a guarantee to harmony. Likewise, in the Philippines, the Priests Ulama Gathering has united Christian and Muslim strict pioneers to advance harmony and address the main drivers of contention in the locale.

In spite of the positive effect of interfaith exchange and harmony drives, different difficulties frustrate their adequacy. One huge snag is the ingenuity of strict fanaticism and fundamentalism, which can fuel narrow mindedness and brutality. Fanatic philosophies frequently reject the possibility of exchange and view other confidence customs as dangers, making it hard to participate in significant discussions. Tending to fanaticism requires a diverse methodology that joins safety efforts with endeavors to counter radicalization and advance moderate voices inside strict networks.

Another test is the absence of institutional help for interfaith drives in certain locales. Despite political precariousness, monetary difficulty, and social agitation, state run administrations might focus on quick worries over long haul endeavors to advance interfaith comprehension. Building institutional systems that help and support interfaith discourse is essential for guaranteeing its congruity and effect.

Besides, authentic complaints and well established hatreds between strict networks can obstruct the advancement of interfaith discourse. At times, well established clashes have made a tradition of doubt and hatred, making it hard for networks to participate in open and helpful exchange. Beating these verifiable strains requires persistence, compassion, and a pledge to tending to the main drivers of enmity.

The job of ladies in interfaith exchange is another region that requires consideration. In numerous conventional settings, ladies' voices might be underestimated or rejected from formal interfaith conversations. In any case, the consideration of ladies is fundamental for an exhaustive and comprehensive exchange that mirrors the variety of strict networks. Endeavors to engage ladies inside strict practices and include them in interfaith drives can add to a more all encompassing and fair way to deal with discourse.

In spite of these difficulties, interfaith exchange and harmony drives hold colossal potential for building an additional comprehensive and open minded world. One critical part of their viability lies in the instructive component of advancing strict proficiency and understanding. Instructive projects that show various religions, their chronicles, and their center convictions can add to dispersing generalizations and cultivating a climate of regard and acknowledgment. Schools, colleges, and strict organizations all assume imperative parts in forming perspectives towards variety and advancing interfaith comprehension since the beginning.

Notwithstanding instruction, interfaith drives benefit from grassroots endeavors that unite individuals at the local area level. Interfaith discourse isn't exclusively the space of strict pioneers or researchers; it includes people from assorted foundations taking part in discussions, sharing encounters, and pursuing shared objectives. Local area based drives that elevate interfaith participation add to building extensions of understanding and trust among individuals of various strict foundations.

Moreover, innovation has arisen as an amazing asset for working with interfaith discourse on a worldwide scale. Web-based entertainment stages, online gatherings, and virtual meetings empower people from various regions of the planet to participate in discussions about their confidence, share points of view, and team up on projects. The computerized domain gives a space to discourse that rises above geological limits and considers a more different and comprehensive trade of thoughts.

Interfaith discourse and harmony drives likewise track down help from global associations and intergovernmental bodies. The Assembled Countries, for instance, perceives the job of strict pioneers and associations in advancing harmony and has started different projects to work with interfaith exchange. The Partnership of Civic establishments, an UN drive, attempts to work on understanding and collaboration among various societies and religions, stressing the significance of discourse in tending to worldwide difficulties.

All in all, interfaith exchange and harmony drives are fundamental parts of the journey for an additional agreeable and bound together world. By cultivating figuring out, advancing coordinated effort, and tending to the underlying drivers of contentions, these drives add to building spans across strict partitions. While challenges persevere, the potential for positive change through interfaith exchange is critical. Training, grassroots endeavors, mechanical progressions, and global help all assume significant parts in propelling the reason for interfaith comprehension and collaboration. In a world set apart by variety, the advancement of discourse among various confidence customs remains as an encouraging sign for a future portrayed by resistance, regard, and tranquil concurrence.

5.1 Examining Jerusalem as a focal point for interfaith dialogue.

Jerusalem, a city saturated with history and strict importance, remains as a point of convergence for interfaith exchange because of its exceptional situation at the intersection of Judaism, Christianity, and Islam. The old city isn't just an actual locus of strict variety yet in addition an image of shared legacy and challenged stories. Analyzing Jerusalem inside the setting of interfaith discourse permits us to dive into the intricacies, difficulties, and possibilities intrinsic in cultivating getting it and participation among followers of these major monotheistic religions.

According to a verifiable point of view, Jerusalem holds a focal spot in the strict stories of Judaism, Christianity, and Islam. It is frequently alluded to as the blessed city, and its strict significance is highlighted by the presence of sacrosanct destinations adored by every practice. For Jews, the Western Wall, a leftover of the old Sanctuary, is a position of petition and journey. Christians partner Jerusalem with the life, demise, and restoration of Jesus Christ, with the Congregation of the Heavenly Tomb denoting the customary site of his torturous killing and entombment. Muslims hold the Al-Aqsa Mosque in high regard, thinking of it as the third holiest site in Islam, related with the Prophet Muhammad's night process.

This combination of strict importance has made Jerusalem a point of convergence for interfaith discourse. The city's common hallowed spaces and interconnected narratives give an unmistakable setting to conversations about shared traits and contrasts among the three confidence customs. Interfaith exchange in Jerusalem frequently includes strict pioneers, researchers, and experts participating in discussions pointed toward developing figuring out, scattering confusions, and encouraging cooperation. The common spaces, in spite of their particular strict affiliations, act as meeting places where people from various confidence foundations can meet up out of a sense of regard and shared investigation.

Be that as it may, the strict meaning of Jerusalem likewise adds to its mind boggling and challenged nature, introducing difficulties to interfaith discourse. The city has been a verifiable and contemporary flashpoint for clashes established in strict, political, and nationalistic strains. The Israeli-Palestinian struggle, with its well established verifiable complaints, has frequently poured out over into strict talk, intensifying divisions and ruining productive discourse. The situation with Jerusalem as the capital of Israel and its challenged nature have been central disputed matters in harmony talks, adding a layer of intricacy to interfaith communications.

One test in interfaith exchange in Jerusalem is exploring the different verifiable stories and understandings of strict occasions. Different strict networks frequently have particular points of view on the city's past, which can add to common errors and support verifiable complaints. The test isn't simply philosophical however stretches out to the sociopolitical domain, where contending stories might fuel hatreds and thwart joint effort. Tending to these disparate stories requires a nuanced approach that recognizes verifiable intricacies while looking for shared view for shared yearnings of harmony and conjunction.

The international real factors of Jerusalem additionally influence the elements of interfaith discourse. The city's division into East and West Jerusalem, with the previous overwhelmingly Palestinian and the last transcendently Jewish, adds a layer of intricacy to interfaith collaborations. Political and social elements shape the regular routines of inhabitants and impact their impression of one another. Conquering these divisions and encouraging discourse across the international limits of Jerusalem requires deliberate endeavors to make spaces for connection and understanding.

Endeavors to advance interfaith exchange in Jerusalem frequently include drives that go past religious conversations to address shared social difficulties. Issues like destitution, instruction, and medical care give shared view to joint effort among strict networks. Interfaith tasks that intend to work on the personal satisfaction for all occupants, independent of their strict foundation, add to building trust and cultivating a feeling of shared liability. By zeroing in on commonsense, unmistakable objectives, interfaith drives in Jerusalem can rise above philosophical contrasts and address the prompt requirements of the assorted populace.

The job of strict forerunners in Jerusalem is urgent in progressing interfaith discourse. Strict figures employ huge impact in molding the points of view of their networks and can assume a key part in advancing resilience and understanding. Interfaith endeavors frequently include cooperative ventures started by strict pioneers, stressing shared values and a guarantee to the prosperity of the whole local area. By utilizing their ethical power, strict pioneers can add to making an air helpful for discourse and collaboration.

Instructive drives likewise assume a urgent part in encouraging interfaith figuring out in Jerusalem. Schools and strict foundations can consolidate educational plans that advance strict proficiency, showing understudies the convictions, practices, and narratives of various confidence customs. Openness to different viewpoints since the beginning can assist with dispersing generalizations and bias, laying the basis for a more comprehensive and lenient society. Also, instructive projects that unite understudies from various strict foundations give open doors to special interactions and fellowships to create, separating obstructions that might exist among networks.

Interfaith discourse in Jerusalem isn't restricted to formal conversations yet frequently reaches out to social trade and shared strict practices. Celebrations, craftsmanship displays, and melodic occasions that praise the variety of strict customs add to building scaffolds of understanding. The common social legacy of Jerusalem gives a rich embroidery that can be woven into the texture of interfaith cooperations, cultivating appreciation for the creative, culinary, and semantic commitments of every local area.

In spite of the difficulties, there have been cases of effective interfaith drives in Jerusalem that deal looks at trust and progress. Associations like the Jerusalem Intercultural Center and Kids4Peace pursue uniting youngsters from various strict foundations, furnishing them with valuable open doors for discourse, fellowship, and joint effort. These drives perceive the extraordinary capability of connecting with the more youthful age in interfaith discourse, as they are the future chiefs and powerhouses who can shape the direction of Jerusalem's social and strict scene.

All in all, looking at Jerusalem as a point of convergence for interfaith exchange uncovers both the intricacies and possibilities inborn in cultivating understanding and coordinated effort among devotees of Judaism, Christianity, and Islam. The city's verifiable and strict importance gives a substantial setting to discourse, while its challenged nature and international real factors present provokes that request deliberate endeavors to survive. Interfaith exchange in Jerusalem should explore disparate authentic accounts, address contemporary socio-political divisions, and include strict pioneers, instructive organizations, and grassroots drives.

Endeavors to advance interfaith comprehension in Jerusalem go past philosophical conversations to envelop shared social difficulties and cooperative activities that benefit the whole local area. Strict pioneers assume a significant part in molding the story and making an environment helpful for exchange, while instructive drives add to separating generalizations and cultivating inclusivity since the beginning. Social trade and shared strict practices further enhance the embroidery of interfaith associations in Jerusalem, giving open doors to networks to praise their variety.

While the difficulties are impressive, the potential for positive change in Jerusalem through interfaith exchange is huge. The city's exceptional situation as a gathering point for various confidence customs offers a stage for building spans, cultivating common regard, and imagining a future set apart by harmony and concurrence. As endeavors keep on tending to verifiable complaints, explore political intricacies, and advance getting it, Jerusalem remains as an image of the common humankind that rises above strict limits and coaxes towards an eventual fate of concordance and solidarity.

5.2 Highlighting efforts and initiatives aimed at promoting peace and understanding among different religious communities.

Endeavors and drives pointed toward advancing harmony and understanding among various strict networks have acquired expanding importance in our interconnected world. As strict variety turns into a main quality of numerous social orders, encouraging exchange and collaboration among different confidence customs becomes basic for the advancement of resilience, shared regard, and tranquil concurrence. This talk plans to investigate the different cluster of endeavors and drives overall that add to building spans among strict networks, underlining the significance of coordinated effort, training, and grassroots developments.

One outstanding road for advancing interfaith comprehension is through coordinated exchanges and gatherings that unite delegates from various strict practices. These occasions give a stage to open and conscious correspondence, permitting members to investigate shared values, moral standards, and shared objectives. Global gatherings, like the Parliament of the World's Religions, consistently assemble strict pioneers, researchers, and experts to take part in significant discussions about harmony, equity, and ecological stewardship. The point isn't to homogenize strict customs yet to see the value in their variety while perceiving the shared view that can act as an establishment for coordinated effort.

Notwithstanding worldwide gatherings, various neighborhood and local interfaith drives assume a fundamental part in encouraging comprehension and collaboration. Interfaith exchange gatherings, frequently worked with by strict pioneers or local area coordinators, make spaces for people from various confidence foundations to meet up in an air of common regard. These drives urge members to share their convictions, practices, and encounters, advancing a more profound comprehension of the wealth and variety of strict customs inside a given local area.

Strict pioneers, given their impact and moral power, assume a critical part in progressing interfaith comprehension. Numerous drives include pastorate from different beliefs taking part in joint exercises, giving joint proclamations, and partaking in shared love administrations. These cooperative endeavors exhibit fortitude among strict pioneers as well as send a strong message of solidarity and collaboration to their separate networks. The contribution of strict pioneers is especially huge in districts set apart by strict strain, where their impact can assist with stopping clashes and advance compromise.

Instructive drives address one more key road for advancing interfaith comprehension. Schools, colleges, and strict organizations can integrate educational programs that stress strict proficiency, showing understudies different confidence customs, their chronicles, and their center convictions. The goal is to disperse generalizations, counter bias, and cultivate a climate where various strict points of view are regarded. Interfaith schooling points not exclusively to grant information yet in addition to develop a mentality of receptiveness and interest, empowering people to draw in with others from a sense of common learning.

Interfaith assistance projects that address social issues and helpful worries give functional open doors to cooperation among strict networks. Whether it's tending to destitution, advancing medical services, or answering cataclysmic events, joint endeavors to lighten enduring rise above strict contrasts and underscore shared upsides of sympathy and equity. Drives like Environment for Humankind, where volunteers from various strict foundations meet up to construct homes for those out of luck, epitomize how cooperative activity can fabricate extensions and encourage a feeling of shared liability regarding the prosperity of society.

Grassroots developments and local area based associations assume a critical part in advancing interfaith comprehension at the nearby level. These drives frequently rise up out of the ground up, driven by people and networks focused on building associations across strict lines. The URI (Joined Religions Drive), for example, is a worldwide grassroots organization that unites individuals from various religions to deal with normal undertakings advancing harmony, equity, and recuperating the Earth. These drives influence the strength of neighborhood networks to make positive change and add to a more extensive culture of understanding and regard.

Media and innovation likewise assume a huge part in forming discernments and encouraging interfaith comprehension. Positive depictions of strict variety in movies, TV, and online stages can challenge generalizations and advance a more nuanced comprehension of various confidence customs. Web-based entertainment, specifically, gives a stage to people to share their own accounts, take part in discussions, and construct virtual networks that rise above geological limits. Virtual interfaith exchanges, online classes, and online gatherings empower people from various regions of the planet to interface and take part in discussions about their confidence, separating obstructions and cultivating a worldwide feeling of local area.

Government and intergovernmental drives add to the advancement of interfaith comprehension by making approaches and systems that help strict variety and safeguard the privileges of people from different confidence foundations. Now and again, legislatures lay out interfaith boards or panels that unite delegates from various strict networks to prompt on issues connected with strict opportunity, social attachment, and local area relations. These drives signal a pledge to cultivating a comprehensive society where people are allowed to rehearse their confidence unafraid of separation.

Interfaith drives are especially important in districts set apart by authentic or continuous strict contentions. In struggle zones, endeavors to advance harmony and seeing frequently include compromise processes that unite agents from clashing strict networks. Truth and compromise commissions, enlivened by effective models, for example, South Africa's post-politically-sanctioned racial segregation commission, mean to address past treacheries, advance mending, and fabricate an establishment for serene conjunction. These drives perceive the job of strict stories in clashes and try to change them into accounts of figuring out, absolution, and shared mankind.

The job of ladies in interfaith exchange is earning expanding respect as a fundamental element of encouraging comprehension and coordinated effort. Ladies frequently assume key parts inside strict networks and can be strong problem solvers in advancing harmony. Drives that enable ladies inside strict practices and include them in interfaith exercises add to a more all encompassing and comprehensive way to deal with discourse. The Ladies of Confidence Peacebuilding Organization, for instance, unites ladies from various strict foundations to work cooperatively on peacebuilding drives, perceiving the extraordinary commitments ladies can reconcile and understanding.

While the endeavors and drives pointed toward advancing harmony and understanding among various strict networks are assorted and diverse, they are not without challenges. One critical test is defeating firmly established biases and generalizations that might endure inside networks. Misinterpretations about other confidence customs can impede certifiable discourse and collaboration, requiring purposeful endeavors to address these inclinations through schooling and relational communications.

Strict fanaticism and fundamentalism address one more impressive test to interfaith comprehension. Fanatic philosophies frequently reject the possibility of exchange and view other confidence customs as dangers, making it challenging to take part in significant discussions. Tending to fanaticism requires an exhaustive methodology that joins safety efforts with endeavors to counter radicalization and advance moderate voices inside strict networks.

Now and again, political and social settings make hindrances to interfaith drives. State run administrations might focus on prompt worries over long haul endeavors to advance interfaith comprehension, and political flimsiness can intensify strict strains. Building institutional structures that help and support interfaith exchange is essential for guaranteeing its coherence and effect, particularly in areas where the political environment may not be helpful for such drives.

All in all, endeavors and drives pointed toward advancing harmony and understanding among various strict networks assume a significant part in cultivating a more open minded, comprehensive, and amicable world. From coordinated exchanges and gatherings to grassroots developments, schooling, and cooperative assistance projects, these drives influence different ways to deal with assemble spans across strict partitions. The contribution of strict pioneers, ladies, legislatures, and the media adds layers of impact and effect on these endeavors.

While challenges persevere, the aggregate obligation to interfaith comprehension flags an acknowledgment of the common mankind that rises above strict limits. The continuous work of people and associations overall mirrors a commitment to making an existence where strict variety is praised, and joint effort among various confidence customs turns into a foundation of quiet conjunction. As these endeavors proceed to develop and grow, the potential for positive change in cultivating interfaith comprehension stays critical, offering expect a future set apart by concordance, regard, and shared values.

5.3 Discussing the challenges and successes of interfaith collaboration in Jerusalem.

Jerusalem, a city venerated by three significant monotheistic religions - Judaism, Christianity, and Islam - remains as a microcosm of strict variety and verifiable importance. The intricate embroidery of its strict legacy has made Jerusalem both an image of solidarity and a flashpoint for strains, making interfaith cooperation inside the city an imposing test. This conversation dives into the multi-layered scene of interfaith joint effort in Jerusalem, analyzing the difficulties it faces and the victories it has accomplished in cultivating figuring out, resistance, and participation among various strict networks.

Challenges in Interfaith Cooperation in Jerusalem:
Authentic Complaints and Stories:

One of the essential difficulties in interfaith cooperation in Jerusalem is the presence of well established authentic complaints and clashing accounts. The city's rich history is a mosaic of victories, occupations, and strict changes. Every strict local area has its own translation of verifiable occasions, which can prompt contending stories that add to pressure and question. Defeating these verifiable complaints requires a fragile methodology that recognizes the different viewpoints while looking for shared conviction for exchange and collaboration.

Political and International Setting:

The international setting of Jerusalem adds an extra layer of intricacy to interfaith coordinated effort. The city has been at the focal point of the Israeli-Palestinian clash, with contending nationalistic desires and claims to sway. The political and regional questions have frequently poured out over into strict aspects, further confusing interfaith communications. Political unsteadiness and the more extensive Center East clash establish a climate where strict cooperation might be impeded by bigger international contemplations.

Strict Fanaticism and Fundamentalism:

The presence of strict radicalism and fundamentalism represents a critical test to interfaith cooperation in Jerusalem. Fanatic philosophies that reject the possibility of concurrence with other confidence customs can subvert endeavors to fabricate extensions and encourage understanding. The impact of revolutionary components inside strict networks might restrict the space for open discourse and collaboration, as people and gatherings upholding radical perspectives might oppose drawing in with those from various confidence foundations.

Asset Portion and Institutional Help:

Interfaith cooperation requires assets, both with regards to financing and institutional help. In Jerusalem, where political and strict awarenesses are high, getting monetary and hierarchical support for interfaith drives can challenge. Legislatures, both neighborhood and worldwide, may confront contending needs, and establishments advancing interfaith discourse might battle to get supported help. The absence of institutional support can block the progression and effect of cooperative endeavors.

Financial Incongruities:

Financial abberations among various strict networks in Jerusalem add to difficulties in cooperation. Financial and social disparities can make pressures and enmities, making it hard for networks to meet up out of a feeling of collaboration. Interfaith drives that plan to address shared social difficulties might confront obstruction on the off chance that the hidden financial inconsistencies are not enough recognized and tended to.

Achievements in Interfaith Cooperation in Jerusalem:
Interfaith Exchanges and Drives:

In spite of the difficulties, Jerusalem has seen effective interfaith exchanges and drives that unite strict pioneers, researchers, and professionals. Gatherings, for example, the Ruler Abdullah container Abdulaziz Worldwide Place for Interreligious and Intercultural Exchange (KAICIID) give a stage to continuous discussions among strict pioneers from different confidence customs. These discoursed center around normal qualities, shared concerns, and potential open doors for coordinated effort, cultivating a feeling of understanding and regard.

Joint Love and Shared Strict Practices:

Effective interfaith cooperation in Jerusalem frequently includes joint love and shared strict practices. Drives that bring people from various confidence customs together for supplication, reflection, or strict ceremonies set out open doors for unique interactions and shared understanding. Shared strict encounters can add to separating obstructions and cultivating a feeling of solidarity among different networks.

Interfaith Assistance Tasks:

Interfaith help projects have demonstrated to find success in advancing coordinated effort among various strict networks in Jerusalem. Drives that address normal social difficulties, like neediness, vagrancy, and medical care, give a viable setting to collaboration. Interfaith help projects not just add to the prosperity of the local area yet in addition exhibit the common upsides of sympathy and social obligation that rise above strict contrasts.

Instructive Drives:

Training assumes an essential part in encouraging interfaith comprehension, and fruitful drives in Jerusalem center around advancing strict proficiency and resistance. Instructive projects that show different confidence customs, their chronicles, and their commitments to culture and society add to dissipating generalizations and building scaffolds of understanding.

Interfaith instructive drives frequently include coordinated effort between schools, colleges, and strict organizations to make an educational plan that advances a more nuanced comprehension of different strict viewpoints.

Social Trade and Expressions Drives:

Social trade and expressions drives have been fruitful in advancing interfaith joint effort in Jerusalem. Celebrations, craftsmanship presentations, and melodic occasions that commend the assorted social and imaginative articulations of various strict networks make spaces for discourse and appreciation. These drives add to building spans by featuring the common social legacy of Jerusalem's inhabitants.

Ladies' Contribution in Interfaith Exercises:

Perceiving the remarkable job that ladies can play in advancing harmony and understanding, effective interfaith drives in Jerusalem include the dynamic support of ladies. Ladies' associations and organizations, for example, the Jerusalem Ladies' Strengthening Organization, unite ladies from various strict foundations to work cooperatively on peacebuilding drives. The contribution of ladies adds an unmistakable viewpoint and adds to a more comprehensive and all encompassing way to deal with interfaith coordinated effort.

Worldwide Help and Discretion:

Global associations and strategic endeavors play had an impact in supporting interfaith coordinated effort in Jerusalem. Drives drove by associations like the Unified Countries and political endeavors by different nations mean to establish a climate helpful for exchange and participation. Worldwide help gives a more extensive structure to interfaith drives and highlights the worldwide meaning of encouraging comprehension and harmony in Jerusalem.

Youth Commitment in Interfaith Exchange:

Perceiving the significance of connecting with the more youthful age, effective interfaith drives in Jerusalem center around youth contribution. Associations like Kids4Peace unite youngsters from various strict foundations, furnishing them with open doors for exchange, fellowship, and cooperative undertakings. Youth commitment adds to building an establishment for future pioneers who are focused on advancing resilience and understanding.

All in all, the difficulties and triumphs of interfaith cooperation in Jerusalem mirror the many-sided elements of a city with significant strict, verifiable, and international aspects. The difficulties, established in authentic complaints, political intricacies, and financial abberations, feature the requirement for nuanced and supported endeavors. In any case, the victories, clear in interfaith discoursed, joint love, administration projects, instructive drives, social trade, ladies' association, global help, and youth commitment, exhibit the flexibility of cooperative endeavors in cultivating understanding and solidarity among various strict networks.

As Jerusalem keeps on exploring its mind boggling reality, these victories give an establishment to trust and the chance of a future where interfaith cooperation isn't just a test yet a groundbreaking power for harmony and conjunction in this holy city.

Interfaith cooperation in Jerusalem, a city holy to Judaism, Christianity, and Islam, is both a convincing yearning and an imposing test. The authentic, strict, and international meaning of Jerusalem adds layers of intricacy to endeavors pointed toward encouraging grasping, resistance, and collaboration among different strict networks. This conversation investigates the elements of interfaith joint effort in Jerusalem, digging into its intricacies, featuring the difficulties it faces, and perceiving the triumphs that have arisen chasing serene concurrence.

Verifiable and Strict Importance:

Jerusalem's verifiable and strict importance is fundamental to grasping the intricacies of interfaith joint effort in the city. For Jews, Jerusalem is the profound focus, with the Western Wall and the remainders of the antiquated Sanctuary holding profound strict importance. Christians venerate Jerusalem as the site of key occasions in the existence of Jesus Christ, including the Torturous killing and Revival, as represented by the Congregation of the Blessed Catacomb. Muslims think about Jerusalem the third holiest city, with the Al-Aqsa Mosque holding unmistakable quality as the site of Prophet Muhammad's night process.

This combination of strict significance establishes an interesting climate where different confidence customs meet, and shared hallowed spaces exist together. In any case, it additionally adds to verifiable complaints, as every strict local area deciphers the city's set of experiences through its own focal point. Defeating these firmly established stories turns into a major test in encouraging interfaith cooperation.

Challenges in Interfaith Cooperation in Jerusalem:
Verifiable Complaints and Contending Stories:

The verifiable embroidered artwork of Jerusalem is woven with successes, occupations, and strict changes. Every strict local area has an unmistakable story, frequently entwined with verifiable complaints and cases to sacrosanct spaces. Contending translations of authentic occasions can prompt doubt and block endeavors to settle on some mutual interest. Spanning these stories requires a fragile methodology that recognizes different viewpoints while looking for shared values and yearnings.

Political and International Elements:

The international setting of Jerusalem, especially with regards to the Israeli-Palestinian struggle, adds layers of intricacy to interfaith joint effort. The city's political status is a longstanding wellspring of dispute, and the more extensive provincial clash frequently spills into strict aspects. The interlacing of political and strict contemplations makes it trying to isolate interfaith cooperation from the bigger international scene.

Strict Fanaticism and Fundamentalism:

The presence of strict fanaticism represents a critical test to interfaith coordinated effort in Jerusalem. Radical belief systems reject the possibility of conjunction and view other confidence customs as dangers. The impact of revolutionary components inside strict networks can prevent open discourse and participation. Countering radicalism requires a multi-layered approach that tends to main drivers while advancing a story of resistance and understanding.

Asset Portion and Institutional Help:

Interfaith cooperation requires assets, both monetary and hierarchical. Getting supported help for drives in Jerusalem can be trying because of political awarenesses and contending needs. Establishments advancing interfaith exchange might battle to keep up with congruity without reliable sponsorship. The absence of institutional help can restrict the effect and extent of cooperative endeavors.

Financial Abberations:

Financial differences among various strict networks add to difficulties in coordinated effort. Financial and social disparities can make pressures, making it challenging for networks to meet up. Drives that don't address hidden abberations might confront obstruction, as financial factors frequently cross with strict personality.

Achievements in Interfaith Joint effort in Jerusalem:

Interfaith Exchanges and Drives:

Regardless of the difficulties, Jerusalem has seen effective interfaith exchanges and drives. Gatherings, for example, the Ruler Abdullah container Abdulaziz Worldwide Place for Interreligious and Intercultural Exchange (KAICIID) unite strict pioneers from different religions. These discoursed center around normal qualities and shared concerns, encouraging a feeling of understanding and regard.

Joint Love and Shared Strict Practices:

Fruitful interfaith coordinated effort frequently includes joint love and shared strict practices. Drives that bring people from various confidence customs together for petition, contemplation, or strict ceremonies set out open doors for unique interactions and common comprehension. Shared strict encounters add to separating hindrances and encouraging a feeling of solidarity.

Interfaith Assistance Undertakings:

Interfaith assistance projects have demonstrated fruitful in advancing joint effort in Jerusalem. Drives that address normal social difficulties, like neediness and medical care, give a pragmatic setting to participation. Past representative signals, these ventures exhibit shared upsides of empathy and social obligation.

Instructive Drives:

Training assumes a critical part in cultivating interfaith comprehension. Effective drives center around advancing strict proficiency and resilience. Instructive projects that show different confidence customs, chronicles, and commitments to culture add to dissipating generalizations and building scaffolds of understanding.

Social Trade and Expressions Drives:

Social trade and expressions drives have been fruitful in advancing interfaith cooperation. Celebrations, craftsmanship shows, and melodic occasions that celebrate different social and imaginative articulations make spaces for exchange and appreciation. These drives feature the common social legacy of Jerusalem's occupants.

Ladies' Contribution in Interfaith Exercises:

Perceiving the extraordinary job that ladies can play in advancing harmony, effective drives include dynamic cooperation from ladies. Ladies' associations and organizations unite ladies from various strict foundations to work cooperatively on peacebuilding drives. The inclusion of ladies adds a particular point of view and adds to a more comprehensive methodology.

Global Help and Strategy:

Worldwide associations and political endeavors support interfaith cooperation in Jerusalem. Drives drove by associations like the Assembled Countries intend to establish a climate helpful for discourse and participation. Worldwide help gives a more extensive system to interfaith drives and highlights the worldwide meaning of encouraging comprehension and harmony in Jerusalem.

Youth Commitment in Interfaith Exchange:

Perceiving the significance of drawing in the more youthful age, fruitful drives center around youth association. Associations unite youngsters from various strict foundations, furnishing them with open doors for exchange, kinship, and cooperative ventures. Youth commitment adds to building an establishment for future pioneers focused on advancing resistance.

Looking Forward:

Interfaith coordinated effort in Jerusalem stays a complicated undertaking, molded by verifiable, political, and strict elements. The difficulties are considerable, however the victories highlight the flexibility and potential for positive change. As Jerusalem keeps on exploring its novel reality, the way ahead requires progressing responsibility, nuanced understanding, and supported endeavors from strict pioneers, networks, states, and worldwide associations.

Encouraging interfaith joint effort in Jerusalem requires a comprehensive methodology that tends to verifiable complaints, advances comprehensive training, and recognizes the financial setting.

Expanding on effective drives, future endeavors ought to zero in on enhancing the voices of ladies, connecting with youth, and utilizing human expression and culture to rise above strict limits.

At last, the vision of an amicable Jerusalem lies in the possession of those focused on the goals of figuring out, resistance, and shared mankind. While challenges continue, the triumphs in interfaith coordinated effort enlighten a way ahead, offering expect a future where Jerusalem turns into a signal of solidarity and conjunction, mirroring the wealth of its different strict embroidery.

Chapter 6

Geopolitical Significance

The international meaning of a locale is a mind boggling and complex idea that incorporates political, financial, social, and key aspects. It alludes to the significance of a specific region in the worldwide political scene and the effect it has on global relations. International importance is much of not entirely settled by a mix of topographical area, normal assets, financial strength, military capacities, and verifiable variables. In this far reaching investigation, we will dive into the different parts of international importance and examine how various districts all over the planet shape the course of worldwide undertakings.

Geological area assumes a pivotal part in deciding the international meaning of a district. Closeness to significant waterways, like seas and oceans, can give competitive edges to exchange, transportation, and military exercises. Beach front districts frequently have simpler admittance to worldwide transportation courses, making them central participants in worldwide trade. Moreover, nations arranged at intersection of significant land courses might become fundamental center points for overland exchange and transportation.

One perfect representation of the international meaning of topographical area is the Center East. This locale, frequently alluded to as the "junction of human advancements," is decisively situated at the convergence of Europe, Asia, and Africa. The Center East has been a point of convergence of international rivalry for quite a long time, given its basic situation along significant shipping lanes and its tremendous energy assets, especially oil. The control and impact over these assets have made the Center East a central participant in worldwide governmental issues, with significant powers competing for predominance and looking to get their inclinations in the locale.

Normal assets are one more essential figure deciding international importance. Areas enriched with plentiful and important assets, like oil, gaseous petrol, minerals, and arable land, frequently hold influence in worldwide issues. Command over these assets adds to financial strength as well as gives influence in global relations. Countries that are significant exporters of key products can impact worldwide business sectors and use huge political power.

The Cold district is a contemporary illustration of the international meaning of normal assets. As environmental change speeds up, the liquefying of Cold ice opens up additional opportunities for asset extraction, especially as far as oil and petroleum gas saves. The Cold's essential significance has expanded as countries seek admittance to these assets, prompting elevated international pressures in the area. Nations with Cold shores, like Russia, Canada, the US, and Nordic countries, are effectively stating their cases and interests in this asset rich region.

Monetary strength is a crucial part of international importance. Countries with powerful and various economies frequently assume a focal part in molding worldwide monetary strategies and exchange elements. Monetary power converts into political impact, as nations that are key part in the worldwide economy can shape global foundations, set exchange guidelines, and impact the way of behaving of different countries.

China's ascent to financial conspicuousness in the late twentieth and mid 21st hundreds of years embodies the international meaning of monetary strength. As the world's second-biggest economy, China's monetary impact broadens universally. Its gigantic assembling capacities, mechanical headways, and huge customer market make it a vital participant in worldwide exchange and venture. China's monetary clout has reshaped worldwide stockpile chains as well as prompted shifts in international arrangements as nations try to lay out financial organizations and partnerships.

Military capacities are a basic determinant of international importance, as countries with impressive military can state their inclinations and impact the overall influence in their particular locales. Military strength fills in as a hindrance against possible enemies and permits countries to extend power past their boundaries. Vital army installations, maritime armadas, and flying corps capacities add to a country's international standing and its capacity to shape territorial and worldwide security elements.

The US, with its unmatched military capacities, has for some time been a prevailing power in molding worldwide international relations. Its broad organization of army installations all over the planet, atomic capacities, and innovative predominance have situated it as the world's transcendent military power. The projection of U.S. military power plays had a significant impact in molding global contentions, peacekeeping endeavors, and the general overall influence in various locales.

Verifiable factors likewise assume a critical part in deciding international importance. The tradition of previous occasions, clashes, and coalitions shapes the ongoing international scene and impacts the connections between countries. Verifiable complaints, regional debates, and the memory of past struggles can add to progressing international pressures and contentions.

One illustration of the getting through effect of verifiable elements is what is happening in the South China Ocean. The regional debates among China and its neighbors, including Vietnam, the Philippines, and Taiwan, have profound authentic roots. Claims over sea domains and authentic complaints have prompted uplifted strains in the locale, with contending interests and vital contemplations worsening the intricacy of the international scene.

Local associations and collusions are instrumental in forming the international meaning of a specific region. These associations act as gatherings for participation, coordination, and compromise among part states. They can likewise go about as international alliances, applying aggregate impact on worldwide issues.

The European Association (EU) is a great representation of a provincial association with huge international ramifications. Initially framed to advance monetary collaboration, the EU has developed into a political and key element with impact past its lines. The EU's development, normal international strategy goals, and shared guard drives add to international importance as a firm coalition assumes a critical part in forming European and foreign relations.

The idea of delicate power, promoted by political researcher Joseph Nye, is one more component of international importance. Delicate power alludes to a country's capacity to impact others through fascination and influence instead of compulsion. Social impact, strategic drives, instructive trade programs, and worldwide media presence add to a nation's delicate power.

The US has generally been a significant purveyor of delicate power, with its universally compelling media outlet, advanced education establishments, and social products. American beliefs of a majority rules system, opportunity, and development have resounded around the world, molding worldwide discernments and impacting political turns of events. Delicate power can supplement military and monetary strength, upgrading a country's generally speaking international impact.

International areas of interest are locales described by extreme contest, struggle, or precariousness, frequently because of covering interests, authentic pressures, or international competitions. These areas of interest are central places of worldwide consideration and can have extensive ramifications for global relations.

The Korean Promontory is a well established international area of interest, set apart by the division among North and South Korea. The tradition of the Korean Conflict, progressing atomic pressures, and the international rivalry between adjoining powers, like China, Russia, and the US, add to the locale's importance. The Korean Landmass fills in as an expected flashpoint with the possibility to affect provincial and worldwide security.

The idea of international turns, presented by the mid twentieth century geographer Halford Mackinder, alludes to decisively found locales that hold the way to worldwide power. Mackinder distinguished the "Heartland," a tremendous expanse of land in Eurasia, as the international turn that, whenever controlled, could rule the world. While the particulars of Mackinder's hypothesis have developed, the possibility of international turns stays important in contemporary international relations.

Focal Asia, with its tremendous territory and closeness to significant powers, is in many cases thought about an international turn in the 21st 100 years. The district's importance lies in its energy assets, transport halls, and its job as a cradle zone between Russia, China, and the Center East. The opposition for impact in Focal Asia includes significant powers trying to lay out financial organizations, secure admittance to assets, and attest international impact.

The development of new international entertainers and the rebalancing of force add to the advancing idea of worldwide international affairs. The ascent of non-Western powers, like China, India, Brazil, and Russia, has prompted a multipolar world where numerous focuses of force exist together. This shift difficulties customary international standards and cultivates a more powerful and complex worldwide framework.

China's Belt and Street Drive (BRI) embodies the country's job as another international entertainer. The BRI, an enormous foundation and monetary improvement project spreading over various landmasses, intends to upgrade network and advance financial collaboration. As China puts resources into foundation projects all over the planet, it lays out new international connections and grows its impact in locales basic to worldwide exchange.

Network safety has arisen as a vital component of international importance in the computerized age. Countries with cutting edge digital abilities can apply impact, disturb enemies, and participate in secretive exercises in the virtual domain. Network safety concerns have become fundamental to public safety procedures, with countries putting resources into digital protections and creating hostile digital capacities.

The US and Russia are among the key part in the domain of digital international affairs. Cyberattacks, reconnaissance, and the advancement of hostile digital capacities are fundamental to their international procedures. The rising interconnectedness of the worldwide economy and dependence on computerized foundation make network safety a basic part of present day international contemplations.

Ecological elements, for example, environmental change and asset shortage, are progressively molding international elements. The effect of environmental change on ocean levels, atmospheric conditions, and cataclysmic events can have flowing consequences for weak areas, prompting removal, asset contest, and possible struggles.

The Icy district, going through fast ecological changes because of an Earth-wide temperature boost, is a point of convergence of natural international relations. The softening ice has opened up additional opportunities for asset extraction, transporting courses, and monetary exercises. Simultaneously, it has raised worries about ecological debasement, regional debates, and the likely militarization of the area.

International importance isn't static; it develops because of evolving conditions, worldwide patterns, and the activities of countries. The interconnectedness of the cutting edge world, worked with by innovation and correspondence, has sped up the speed of international change. As countries adjust to new difficulties and open doors, the international scene keeps on moving, introducing the two dangers and opportunities for the global local area.

6.1 Analyzing Jerusalem's geopolitical importance in the modern world.

Jerusalem, with its rich history and profound strict importance, remains at the intersection of international relations, filling in as a point of convergence for local strains and worldwide interests. Dissecting Jerusalem's international significance in the cutting edge world requires a complete assessment of its verifiable setting, strict importance, regional questions, and the more extensive elements that shape the district.

By and large, Jerusalem has been a city of extraordinary importance, filling in as a middle for three significant monotheistic religions: Judaism, Christianity, and Islam. Its Old City, with its notorious destinations like the Western Wall, the Congregation of the Sacred Mausoleum, and the Vault of the Stone, holds huge strict and social significance for billions of individuals around the world. The city's verifiable and strict importance has made it an image of personality and having a place for various networks, adding to its perplexing international elements.

Strict importance, entwined with Jerusalem's set of experiences, assumes a focal part in molding its international significance.

The city's status as a sacred webpage for various religions has prompted contending cases and desires, making a complicated trap of strict and social responsive qualities. The opposition for control and impact over strict destinations has been a wellspring of strain, both inside the city and on the worldwide stage.

The Israeli-Palestinian clash, an extended and well established battle for land, assets, and public character, essentially adds to Jerusalem's international significance. The city's eastern part, involved by Israel during the Six-Day Battle in 1967, stays a point of convergence of conflict among Israelis and Palestinians. The situation with East Jerusalem, guaranteed by Palestinians as the capital of a future state, is a significant disputed matter in harmony discussions and a wellspring of continuous provincial pressures.

The worldwide local area's association in the Israeli-Palestinian struggle further enhances Jerusalem's international importance. Different countries and associations have personal stakes in the goal of the contention, either because of verifiable coalitions, political contemplations, or worries about territorial dependability. The situation with Jerusalem is in many cases a central issue of conversation in discretionary endeavors and worldwide discussions zeroed in on accomplishing an enduring and evenhanded goal to the contention.

One of the center components of Jerusalem's international significance is the city's part in molding Israel's personality and territorial impact. Israel's foundation in 1948 denoted a crucial second in the international affairs of the Center East, prompting a progression of contentions with adjoining Middle Easterner states. Jerusalem, assigned as Israel's capital, turned into an image of the nation's sway and a point of convergence for public pride.

The migration of the U.S. Consulate to Jerusalem in 2018 by the Trump organization added another layer to the city's international importance. The move was praised by Israel as an acknowledgment of its sway over Jerusalem, while it was met with analysis and judgment from numerous in the global local area, especially Middle Easterner and Muslim-greater part nations. The U.S. choice featured the responsiveness of Jerusalem's status and affecting worldwide partnerships and discretionary relations potential.

Jerusalem's international significance isn't restricted to the Israeli-Palestinian clash; it stretches out to the more extensive territorial elements of the Center East. The city's strict importance makes it an emblematic standard for different territorial entertainers, including adjoining Middle Easterner states and non-Bedouin Muslim-larger part countries. Command over or impact in Jerusalem permits countries to declare their remaining in the more extensive Muslim world and shape view of administration in local undertakings.

The complex international scene of the Center East, set apart by authentic contentions, partisan strains, and moving coalitions, further highlights Jerusalem's importance.

The city turns into an international chessboard where provincial powers move to propel their inclinations and impact. The Israeli-Palestinian clash, with Jerusalem at its center, meets with more extensive local elements, making a nexus of interconnected international contemplations.

Iran's job in the Center East adds one more layer to the international intricacy encompassing Jerusalem. As a significant provincial power with key interests and impact across the Center East, Iran has utilized the Israeli-Palestinian clash and Jerusalem's status to energize support among its partners and challenge its foes. The city's representative significance in the Islamic world gives Iran an expository device to speak to more extensive feelings and position itself as a safeguard of Palestinian freedoms.

The international significance of Jerusalem additionally stretches out past the Center East, impacting the elements of global relations. The city's importance in worldwide strict and social legacy reverberates with individuals around the world, making it a subject of interest for countries and networks a long ways past the boundaries of the Center East. Worldwide entertainers, including significant powers and worldwide associations, draw in with the Israeli-Palestinian struggle and Jerusalem's status because of its more extensive ramifications for territorial soundness and worldwide security.

The Unified Countries, as a vital worldwide establishment, has been engaged with different limits in tending to the Israeli-Palestinian struggle and the situation with Jerusalem. Goals and choices by the UN, especially the Security Board, have tried to address the center issues of the contention, including the situation with Jerusalem. The worldwide local area's commitment through the UN mirrors the worldwide acknowledgment of Jerusalem's significance as a consider the more extensive quest for harmony and soundness.

The international relations of Jerusalem additionally converges with the interests of major worldwide powers, especially the US, Russia, and the European Association. These powers, each with its own international contemplations and unions in the Center East, draw in with the Israeli-Palestinian clash and Jerusalem's status in different ways. The contribution of significant powers adds a layer of intricacy to the international scene, as their strategies and positions can shape the course of territorial turns of events.

The situation with Jerusalem isn't just an issue of political and strict importance yet in addition has financial ramifications for the district. The city, as a social and strict the travel industry center, contributes essentially to the economies of Israel and the Palestinian domains. The potential for monetary improvement in Jerusalem, especially with regards to a nonaggression treaty, has been a mark of conversation in different harmony recommendations and discussions. Monetary contemplations further highlight the multi-layered nature of Jerusalem's international significance.

Jerusalem's international importance is additionally entwined with more extensive patterns in worldwide legislative issues, like the ascent of populism, patriotism, and strict personality. These patterns, apparent in various areas of the planet, can impact the stories and strategies encompassing the Israeli-Palestinian clash and Jerusalem's status. The enticement for strict and patriot feelings by political pioneers adds a layer of intricacy to the international contemplations encompassing the city.

All in all, examining Jerusalem's international significance in the cutting edge world requires a nuanced comprehension of its verifiable, strict, and social importance, as well as its job in the Israeli-Palestinian struggle and more extensive territorial elements. The city's status as a heavenly site for different religions, its centrality to the Israeli-Palestinian clash, and its representative significance in worldwide issues make it a point of convergence of international contemplations for countries and global entertainers. The perplexing transaction of verifiable, strict, and international variables highlights the difficulties and open doors related with tending to the situation with Jerusalem and accomplishing a maintainable and fair goal to the more extensive Israeli-Palestinian clash.

6.2 Examining the historical and current political issues surrounding the city.

Analyzing the verifiable and current policy driven issues encompassing the city of Jerusalem requires diving into hundreds of years of mind boggling occasions, clashes, and international elements. This old city holds tremendous strict importance for Judaism, Christianity, and Islam, making it a point of convergence of dispute and discussion in the domain of worldwide governmental issues. Understanding the verifiable setting is pivotal to disentangling the many-sided snare of political provokes that keep on forming the city's predetermination.

By and large, Jerusalem has been a city set apart by successes, strict changes, and social trades. In old times, it filled in as the capital of the Realm of Judah and later turned into a urgent place for early Christianity. The Islamic success in the seventh century carried another part to Jerusalem's set of experiences, making it the third holiest city in Islam. The Campaigns, a progression of middle age strict conflicts, saw the city changing hands among Christian and Muslim rulers, each transforming its scene.

The Ottoman Domain's command over Jerusalem for a really long time, from the mid sixteenth hundred years for the rest of The Second Great War, presented a time of relative dependability. Notwithstanding, the breakdown of the Ottoman Domain after The Second Great War denoted a defining moment in the district's political scene. The Class of Countries conceded England the order to oversee Palestine, including Jerusalem, prompting expanded strains among Jewish and Bedouin people group.

The Assembled Countries' 1947 segment plan proposed the internationalization of Jerusalem, however the ensuing Bedouin Israeli Conflict in 1948 brought about the city being split among Jordanian and Israeli control.

The truce line drawn through the city left West Jerusalem under Israeli control and East Jerusalem, including the Old City, under Jordanian control. This division set up for future contentions and laid the basis for the Israeli-Palestinian battle over the city.

The Six-Day Battle in 1967 denoted a turning point in Jerusalem's set of experiences. Israel's tactical triumph brought about the control of East Jerusalem, including the Old City, and the reunification of the city under Israeli control. The extension of East Jerusalem by Israel was not globally perceived, and the Assembled Countries Security Board passed goals calling for Israel to pull out from the involved regions. The unsettled status of Jerusalem turned into a center issue in the Israeli-Palestinian struggle, with the two sides making a case for the city as their capital.

The issue of Jerusalem acquired reestablished consideration in 1980 when Israel authoritatively proclaimed Jerusalem its "everlasting and unified" capital. The global local area, including the US, didn't embrace this move, keeping up with that the city's last status ought not set in stone through discussions between the gatherings associated with the contention. The continuous policy driven issues encompassing Jerusalem have been a predictable wellspring of strain, hindering harmony endeavors and adding to an environment of doubt and enmity.

The segment sytesis of Jerusalem further confounds the political scene. The city is home to different strict and ethnic networks, including Jewish, Muslim, and Christian populaces. The Old City, with its strict locales, limited back streets, and memorable designs, is a microcosm of this variety. The policy driven issues encompassing Jerusalem are personally associated with the yearnings and complaints of these networks, each competing for acknowledgment, portrayal, and command over their particular blessed destinations.

The Israeli-Palestinian clash, profoundly weaved with the destiny of Jerusalem, has been a determined wellspring of political difficulties in the district. The foundation of the Territory of Israel in 1948 and the ensuing uprooting of Palestinians brought about firmly established complaints and an exile emergency. The issue of Palestinian outcasts, a considerable lot of whom were removed from their homes during the 1948 conflict, stays a center worry in exchanges and a critical hindrance to a complete nonaggression treaty.

The situation with East Jerusalem, especially the Old City with its strict locales, is a basic disputed matter. The Western Wall, respected by Jews as a heavenly site, is situated in the Old City, similar to the Al-Aqsa Mosque, quite possibly of the holiest site in Islam. The Congregation of the Blessed Mausoleum, a key Christian journey site, further adds to the strict intricacy of the area. The covering strict cases and the longing for command over these locales have powered pressures and molded the political scene of Jerusalem.

The Oslo Accords, endorsed during the 1990s, pointed toward laying out a system for settling the Israeli-Palestinian struggle. Notwithstanding, the subject of Jerusalem's last status was conceded to the last phases of dealings. In spite of discontinuous discussions and harmony drives, the situation with Jerusalem stays quite possibly of the most difficult and antagonistic issue, with both Israeli and Palestinian pioneers affirming their freedoms to the city.

The development of settlements in East Jerusalem by Israel has been a wellspring of global analysis and a significant impediment to harmony endeavors. The development of Israeli settlements, thought about unlawful under global regulation, has prompted the uprooting of Palestinian people group and further stressed relations between the gatherings. The settlements not just change the segment creation of East Jerusalem yet in addition influence the regional contiguity of a possible future Palestinian state.

The U.S. acknowledgment of Jerusalem as the capital of Israel in 2017 and the resulting movement of its consulate to the city further aggravated pressures. While Israel invited the move, Palestinians and numerous in the worldwide local area saw it as a takeoff from the well established position that the city's status ought not set in stone through exchanges. The U.S. choice highlighted the responsiveness of Jerusalem as an international flashpoint and impacting worldwide conciliatory relations potential.

The topic of Jerusalem additionally resounds inside the more extensive setting of provincial international relations. Bedouin states, generally went against to Israel's presence, have considered the situation with Jerusalem a litmus test for their relations with Israel. The standardization arrangements among Israel and some Middle Easterner states, known as the Abraham Accords, have presented another powerful in the area. While these arrangements zeroed in on monetary and security collaboration, the issue of Jerusalem stays an emblematic and emotive component that keeps on forming local discernments.

The job of outer entertainers, especially the US, in molding the political scene of Jerusalem couldn't possibly be more significant. The U.S. has been a vital partner of Israel and a go between in the harmony cycle. In any case, its nearby partnership with Israel has prompted wariness and question among Palestinians and some Middle Easterner states. The contribution of outer entertainers in the governmental issues of Jerusalem adds a layer of intricacy, as their strategies and choices have broad ramifications for the locale.

The strict component of Jerusalem's policy driven issues is a focal viewpoint that can't be disregarded. The city's strict locales are images of confidence as well as wellsprings of social personality and verifiable accounts. The control and admittance to these destinations are matters of political discussions as well as contact on firmly established strict responsive qualities. The administration of strict destinations in Jerusalem requires fragile discretion and regard for the strict practices and customs of various networks.

The Unified Countries and different worldwide associations keep on assuming a part in resolving the policy driven issues encompassing Jerusalem. Goals and proclamations from the UN, especially the Security Board and the Overall Gathering, mirror the global local area's position on the city's status. Requires a two-state arrangement and dealings among Israel and the Palestinians to decide the last status of Jerusalem stay key to the worldwide way to deal with the contention.

Lately, considerate society drives, grassroots developments, and individuals to-individuals exchange have acquired unmistakable quality as correlative endeavors to true strategic channels. These drives, including people, associations, and networks, try to cultivate understanding, span isolates, and advance conjunction in Jerusalem. While they may not supplant formal talks, they add to building connections and tending to the human element of the political difficulties confronting the city.

The policy driven issues encompassing Jerusalem are profoundly interconnected with more extensive provincial and worldwide elements. The city's verifiable and strict importance, joined with its part in the Israeli-Palestinian clash, makes it a point of convergence for global consideration and strategic endeavors. The unsettled status of Jerusalem stays an impressive snag to accomplishing an exhaustive and enduring harmony in the district.

All in all, looking at the verifiable and current policy centered issues encompassing Jerusalem requires exploring a complicated landscape molded by hundreds of years of strict, social, and political elements. The city's importance in the Israeli-Palestinian clash, its strict significance, and its job in territorial international affairs add to a complex arrangement of difficulties. The journey for a goal to the policy centered issues encompassing Jerusalem stays one of the basic undertakings in accomplishing a manageable and fair harmony in the Center East.

6.3 Discussing how Jerusalem's geopolitical status influences global politics.

The international status of Jerusalem holds significant ramifications for worldwide legislative issues, rising above territorial limits and impacting the elements of global relations. As one of the most established and most challenged urban communities on the planet, Jerusalem's importance isn't restricted to the Israeli-Palestinian clash; rather, it reverberates on the worldwide stage because of its strict, social, and authentic significance. Breaking down what Jerusalem's international status means for worldwide governmental issues requires an assessment of its effect on key entertainers, territorial dependability, and more extensive discretionary contemplations.

One of the manners by which Jerusalem's international status resounds universally is through its centrality in the Israeli-Palestinian clash.

The unsettled status of Jerusalem stays a center issue in the extended battle among Israelis and Palestinians, molding the story and needs of the worldwide local area. The city's importance as an image of public personality, strict legacy, and regional cases intensifies its effect past the prompt district.

The Unified Countries, as a vital worldwide establishment, has been effectively taken part in tending to the international status of Jerusalem. Goals and proclamations from the UN General Gathering and the Security Committee mirror the worldwide agreement on the significance of settling the city's status through exchanges between the gatherings in question. The worldwide local area's obligation to a two-state arrangement, with Jerusalem as the future capital of both Israel and a Palestinian state, highlights the city's worldwide importance chasing harmony.

The US, as a significant worldwide power and a vital partner of Israel, assumes an essential part in molding the international status of Jerusalem. The U.S. acknowledgment of Jerusalem as the capital of Israel in 2017 and the resulting movement of its consulate to the city denoted a huge takeoff from the well established global agreement. While Israel invited the move, it was met with broad analysis from the Bedouin world and numerous different countries. The U.S. choice to perceive Jerusalem as Israel's capital has suggestions for its job as a go between in the Israeli-Palestinian harmony process and its more extensive impact in the Center East.

The European Association (EU) and its part states have reliably pushed for an arranged settlement to the situation with Jerusalem as a feature of the more extensive Israeli-Palestinian clash. The EU's position lines up with the global agreement that believes Jerusalem's last status to be dependent upon discussions between the gatherings. The EU's discretionary endeavors, proclamations, and monetary commitments to harmony drives add to its job as a worldwide entertainer in tending to the international difficulties related with the city.

Jerusalem's international status additionally crosses with the more extensive pattern of rising populism, patriotism, and strict personality in worldwide governmental issues. The enticement for strict feelings and the outlining of Jerusalem as an image of social legacy reverberate with political developments that focus on public and strict personality. The city's importance turns into a standard for political pioneers looking to energize backing and shape homegrown stories, impacting provincial elements as well as the more extensive flows of worldwide governmental issues.

The job of outer entertainers, past the immediate gatherings associated with the Israeli-Palestinian struggle, further highlights the worldwide elements of Jerusalem's international status. Russia, with verifiable connections to the district and a functioning job in Center East tact, has drawn in with the issue of Jerusalem inside the structure of more extensive local dependability. Russia's collaborations with vital participants, including Israel and Palestine, add to the worldwide international talk encompassing the city.

China's extending worldwide impact has likewise prompted its association in Center East issues, including the Israeli-Palestinian clash and the situation with Jerusalem. As a key part in the worldwide field, China's positions and discretionary commitment shape the talk on worldwide administration and provincial steadiness. Jerusalem's international importance turns out to be essential for China's more extensive contemplations in its way to deal with the Center East.

The Bedouin world, with its verifiable connections to Jerusalem and the Palestinian reason, assumes a urgent part in forming the city's international status on the worldwide stage. The Middle Easterner Association, as a territorial association, has reliably communicated its obligation to the Palestinian reason and upheld for the privileges of Palestinians in

Jerusalem. The Middle Easterner world's strategic endeavors, monetary influence, and social impact add to the more extensive global talk on Jerusalem's international status.

The international significance of Jerusalem is additionally intensified by its job as a strict and social focus. The city's strict locales, including the Western Wall, the Al-Aqsa Mosque, and the Congregation of the Sacred Tomb, draw in travelers and guests from around the world. Strict pioneers and networks overall view Jerusalem as a profound point of convergence, and improvements in the city can possibly reverberate universally, molding discernments and impacting strategic relations.

The situation with Jerusalem likewise crosses with more extensive issues of basic freedoms and worldwide regulation. The development of Israeli settlements in East Jerusalem, thought about unlawful under worldwide regulation, has been a wellspring of worldwide concern and judgment. Common liberties associations and promoters overall have featured the effect of settlement extension on Palestinian people group and the difficulties it postures to the acknowledgment of a two-state arrangement. The worldwide talk on the international status of Jerusalem integrates contemplations of equity, common liberties, and adherence to global legitimate standards.

The city's international status has suggestions for local strength, and its importance is felt in the more extensive setting of the Center East. The unsettled status of Jerusalem adds to pressures among Israel and its Middle Easterner neighbors, influencing provincial elements and coalitions. The city's representative significance as a social and strict standard impacts the insights and strategies of provincial entertainers, molding the more extensive international scene of the Center East.

The standardization arrangements among Israel and some Middle Easterner states, known as the Abraham Accords, address an outstanding improvement with suggestions for Jerusalem's international status. While the arrangements center around financial and security collaboration, they present another discretionary system in the locale. The Abraham Accords, worked with by the US, highlight the developing elements in the Center East and the potential for shifts in provincial coalitions that might have more extensive worldwide implications.

Jerusalem's international status is inseparably connected to the more extensive subject of strict discretion, where countries influence their strict legacy and affiliations to shape worldwide relations. The city's strict importance as a middle for Judaism, Christianity, and Islam permits countries to declare their impact and fabricate collusions in light of shared strict character. This strict discretion stretches out past the Center East, resounding with networks and pioneers overall who view Jerusalem as an image of strict legacy and variety.

The international status of Jerusalem likewise converges with the more extensive difficulties of peacemaking and compromise in the global framework. The city's status as a challenged region with profound verifiable and strict roots presents difficulties that resound with different struggles all over the planet. Illustrations gained from endeavors to address the international difficulties of Jerusalem add to the more extensive talk on compromise, strategy, and the job of worldwide entertainers in encouraging harmony.

The issue of Jerusalem has been a common subject in worldwide discussions and global meetings zeroed in on compromise and peacebuilding. Researchers, representatives, and policymakers participate in conversations about the intricacies of Jerusalem's international status and the illustrations that can be attracted from endeavors to address the Israeli-Palestinian struggle. The city's importance fills in as a contextual investigation in the more extensive scholar and strategy talk on compromise and worldwide relations.

All in all, the international status of Jerusalem applies an extensive impact on worldwide legislative issues, rising above its nearby local setting. The city's authentic, strict, and social importance reverberates with individuals, pioneers, and countries around the world. Jerusalem's effect on worldwide relations is apparent in the strategic endeavors of key entertainers, the goals and explanations of global associations, and the more extensive talk on issues like common freedoms, strict strategy, and compromise. The city's international status fills in as a crystal through which more extensive worldwide elements are refracted, mirroring the interconnectedness of nearby and worldwide legislative issues in the 21st 100 years.

Jerusalem's international status fills in as a nexus of verifiable, strict, and political intricacies, projecting a significant impact on worldwide governmental issues. This old city, loved by three significant monotheistic religions — Judaism, Christianity, and Islam — remains as an image of social legacy, profound importance, and political dispute. As we investigate how Jerusalem's international status resounds on the worldwide stage, it becomes obvious that the city's importance rises above territorial lines, molding conciliatory relations, impacting global associations, and adding to more extensive international elements.

The Israeli-Palestinian clash, with Jerusalem at its center, is a point of convergence of worldwide consideration. The city's status is unpredictably connected to the longstanding battle among Israelis and Palestinians for regional control, self-assurance, and public personality.

The worldwide local area, addressed by associations like the Assembled Countries (UN), has been effectively engaged with tending to the intricacies of the contention, mirroring the worldwide agreement that the last status of Jerusalem ought not entirely settled through discussions between the gatherings.

The UN General Gathering and the Security Board play played focal parts in molding the worldwide talk on Jerusalem. Goals and proclamations from these bodies highlight the worldwide agreement that perceives the city's importance to numerous strict networks and stresses the requirement for an arranged answer for its status. The UN's contribution mirrors a promise to a two-state arrangement, with Jerusalem as the capital of both Israel and a future Palestinian state, highlighting the worldwide significance of settling the city's international difficulties.

The US, as a significant worldwide power and a critical partner of Israel, employs huge impact over the international status of Jerusalem. The choice by the Trump organization in 2017 to perceive Jerusalem as the capital of Israel and move the U.S. government office to the city denoted a takeoff from the longstanding global agreement. While Israel praised the move, it was met with far reaching analysis and judgment, especially from Middle Easterner and Muslim-larger part nations. The U.S. job in molding the international status of Jerusalem features the city's worldwide reverberation and affecting more extensive discretionary relations potential.

On the other hand, the European Association (EU) and its part states have reliably stuck to a place that lines up with the global agreement on Jerusalem's status. The EU advocates for an arranged settlement to the Israeli-Palestinian clash and perceives the city's importance to various strict networks. The EU's conciliatory endeavors, monetary commitments to harmony drives, and accentuation on a two-state arrangement add to its job as a worldwide entertainer in tending to the international difficulties related with Jerusalem.

Russia, with authentic connections to the Center East and dynamic inclusion in local tact, draws in with the international status of Jerusalem as a feature of more extensive endeavors to add to provincial steadiness. Russia's connections with vital participants in the locale, including Israel and Palestine, feature the city's worldwide significance and its job in the more extensive international relations of the Center East. As an extremely durable individual from the UN Security Committee, Russia's position on Jerusalem becomes essential to the worldwide strategic talk on the city's future.

China's developing worldwide impact has prompted its contribution in Center East issues, including the Israeli-Palestinian struggle and the situation with Jerusalem. While China's essential spotlight has been on monetary interests and strategic commitment, its situation on

the international difficulties of Jerusalem adds a layer of intricacy to the worldwide

contemplations of the city's future. China's job mirrors the interconnected idea of contemporary international relations and the extending impact of countries past the quick locale.

The Middle Easterner world, with its verifiable connections to Jerusalem and the Palestinian reason, assumes a pivotal part in forming the city's international status on the worldwide stage. The Middle Easterner Association, as a provincial association, reliably communicates its obligation to the Palestinian reason and supporters for the freedoms of Palestinians in Jerusalem. The Middle Easterner world's political endeavors, monetary influence, and social impact add to the more extensive global talk on Jerusalem's international status.

Jerusalem's international significance reaches out past the limits of the Israeli-Palestinian struggle to converge with the more extensive pattern of rising populism, patriotism, and strict character in worldwide legislative issues. The city's enticement for strict feelings and its representative importance as a social legacy site reverberate with political developments that focus on public and strict personality. Jerusalem turns into a standard for pioneers trying to energize backing and shape homegrown stories, impacting provincial elements as well as the more extensive flows of worldwide legislative issues.

Strict strategy arises as a huge part of Jerusalem's international impact. The city's strict locales, including the Western Wall, the Al-Aqsa Mosque, and the Congregation of the Heavenly Mausoleum, draw in travelers and guests from around the world. Strict pioneers and networks overall view Jerusalem as a profound point of convergence, and improvements in the city can possibly reverberate worldwide, molding discernments and impacting strategic relations.

The international status of Jerusalem converges with more extensive issues of basic freedoms and global regulation. The development of Israeli settlements in East Jerusalem, thought about unlawful under worldwide regulation, has been a wellspring of worldwide concern and judgment. Common freedoms associations and supporters overall feature the effect of settlement development on Palestinian people group and the difficulties it postures to the acknowledgment of a two-state arrangement. The worldwide talk on the international status of

Jerusalem consolidates contemplations of equity, common freedoms, and adherence to global lawful standards.

The unsettled status of Jerusalem adds to strains among Israel and its Middle Easterner neighbors, influencing territorial elements and partnerships. The city's emblematic significance as a social and strict standard impacts the insights and strategies of territorial entertainers, forming the more extensive international scene of the Center East. Provincial steadiness, a critical worry for the global local area, is unpredictably connected to the goal of the international difficulties related with Jerusalem.

The standardization arrangements among Israel and some Middle Easterner states, known as the Abraham Accords, address a striking improvement with suggestions for Jerusalem's international status. While the arrangements center around financial and security collaboration, they present another strategic system in the district. The Abraham Accords, worked with by the US, highlight the developing elements in the Center East and the potential for shifts in provincial coalitions that might have more extensive worldwide repercussions.

Common society drives, grassroots developments, and individuals to-individuals exchange likewise add to the worldwide talk on Jerusalem's international status. These endeavors, including people, associations, and networks, try to cultivate understanding, span partitions, and advance concurrence in Jerusalem. While they may not supplant formal exchanges, they add to building connections and tending to the human element of the political difficulties confronting the city.

The issue of Jerusalem has been a common subject in worldwide discussions and global meetings zeroed in on compromise and peacebuilding. Researchers, negotiators, and policymakers participate in conversations about the intricacies of Jerusalem's international status and the examples that can be attracted from endeavors to address the Israeli-Palestinian clash. The city's importance fills in as a contextual investigation in the more extensive scholar and strategy talk on compromise and worldwide relations.

Chapter 7

Humanitarian and Social Impact

Helpful and social effect are two entwined features of our worldwide presence, winding around a mind boggling embroidery of interconnectedness that rises above lines, societies, and philosophies. At the core of these ideas lies a crucial truth: the innate obligation we share as occupants of this planet to inspire, support, and engage each other.

In looking at philanthropy, we experience a way of thinking grounded in sympathy, compassion, and a pledge to reducing the enduring of individual people. It reaches out past simple foundation, incorporating a comprehensive way to deal with tending to the main drivers of human miscry and supporting for the poise and freedoms of each and every person. Helpful endeavors manifest in a bunch of structures, going from crisis alleviation in the fallout of catastrophic events to long haul improvement projects pointed toward cultivating supportable jobs.

One of the characterizing highlights of compassionate activity is its capacity to cut across international limits. At the point when catastrophe strikes, whether as seismic tremors, floods, or clashes, the basic to answer knows no boundaries. It prompts countries, associations, and people to save contrasts and hold hands in a common mission to mitigate human misery. This common obligation is a demonstration of the interconnectedness of our worldwide local area, highlighting that our aggregate prosperity is dependent upon our capacity to stretch out some assistance to those out of luck.

However, while compassion looks to address quick emergencies and give alleviation, the quest for enduring social effect dives into the complexities of fundamental issues and their hidden causes. Social effect drives are impetuses for change, expecting to change social orders by tending to foundational problems like destitution, disparity, and treachery. These drives frequently work at the crossing point of public, private, and non-benefit areas, perceiving that supportable change requires a multi-layered approach.

Training arises as a foundation in the mission for social effect. Engaging people through admittance to quality instruction upgrades their self-improvement as well as adds to the general advancement of networks and countries. Instruction is an amazing asset for breaking the pattern of neediness, cultivating development, and advancing social union. By putting resources into training, social orders lay the basis for a future where people are furnished with the information and abilities to explore an undeniably complicated world.

Neediness, in any case, stays a considerable boundary to human turn of events and a point of convergence for both helpful and social effect endeavors. It is a diverse peculiarity with sweeping ramifications, influencing admittance to essential necessities like food, medical services, and haven. Social effect drives frequently utilize a granular perspective, drawing in with networks to co-make arrangements that address the particular difficulties they face. Microfinance programs, professional preparation, and local area drove improvement projects are instances of mediations intended to enable people and networks to lift themselves out of destitution.

Chasing social effect, orientation balance remains as a non-debatable standard. The strengthening of ladies and the destroying of orientation based separation are moral goals as well as essential activities for cultural advancement. Whenever ladies are offered equivalent chances in training, business, and navigation, social orders prosper. Perceiving the groundbreaking force of orientation fairness, social effect drives endeavor to separate settled in standards and foundational obstructions that sustain orientation variations.

Natural supportability is one more basic component of social effect. The interconnectedness between human prosperity and the strength of the planet is progressively apparent. Environmental change, deforestation, and contamination are worldwide difficulties that request aggregate activity. Social effect drives that attention on natural supportability look to accommodate human improvement with environmental protection. Through imaginative arrangements and local area commitment, these drives plan to make an agreeable equilibrium that guarantees the prosperity of both present and people in the future.

In the computerized age, innovation arises as a strong device for driving social effect. The approach of data and correspondence innovations has reformed the manner in which we associate, team up, and address cultural difficulties.

From versatile wellbeing applications that improve medical care availability to online instruction stages that democratize learning, innovation can possibly enhance the effect of social drives. Notwithstanding, it is fundamental to guarantee that the advantages of innovation are comprehensive and arrive at minimized networks, forestalling the intensification of existing imbalances.

In the domain of philanthropy, the significance of successful correspondence couldn't possibly be more significant. Emergencies request quick and facilitated reactions, requiring clear channels of correspondence between help associations, legislatures, and impacted networks. Virtual entertainment, specifically, has arisen as an incredible asset for dispersing data, preparing backing, and giving voice to the individuals who frequently go unheard. Nonetheless, the advanced scene additionally presents difficulties, including the spread of deception and the potential for computerized partitions to reject specific populaces from fundamental correspondence organizations.

The displaced person emergency fills in as a powerful illustration of the convergence among philanthropy and social effect. Constrained dislodging, whether because of contention, mistreatment, or ecological elements, presents an intricate test that requires extensive and supportable arrangements. Helpful endeavors give quick alleviation, offering safe house, food, and clinical help to those dislodged. At the same time, social effect drives address the drawn out coordination and prosperity of displaced people, perceiving their strength and likely commitments to have social orders.

Sympathy is the key part that ties philanthropy and social effect together. It is the capacity to comprehend and discuss the thoughts of others, rising above social, phonetic, and geological obstructions. Sympathy isn't simply a feeling however a main impetus that urges people and associations to make a significant move. The impetus for volunteers race to calamity stricken regions, for policymakers who advocate for comprehensive strategies, and for pioneers who devise answers for squeezing cultural difficulties.

As we explore the intricacies of the 21st 100 years, the significance of a worldwide viewpoint turns out to be progressively obvious. The difficulties we face — from worldwide wellbeing emergencies to environmental change — rise above public boundaries. In this interconnected world, the quest for compassionate and social effect requires coordinated effort on an extraordinary scale. Global participation, directed by the standards of value and equity, is fundamental for creating viable answers for shared difficulties.

The Unified Countries, with its Supportable Improvement Objectives (SDGs), remains as a demonstration of the worldwide obligation to resolving the most major problems confronting humankind. These objectives give a guide to aggregate activity, enveloping goals, for example, killing destitution, guaranteeing quality schooling, advancing orientation uniformity, and cultivating natural maintainability.

The SDGs act as a binding together structure that adjusts philanthropic and social effect endeavors, stressing the interconnectedness of different objectives and the requirement for comprehensive arrangements.

Chasing after helpful and social effect, the job of organizations and partnerships can't be ignored. Past the customary worldview of benefit driven thought processes, there is a developing acknowledgment of the obligation that organizations bear in adding to cultural prosperity. Corporate social obligation (CSR) has developed from a charitable extra to a vital piece of business systems. Organizations are progressively adjusting their activities to moral standards, perceiving that manageable strategic policies are great for society as well as for long haul monetary reasonability.

The idea of shared esteem, as expressed by Michael Watchman and Imprint Kramer, highlights that cultural advancement and business achievement are not fundamentally unrelated. By tending to cultural requirements through their center business exercises, organizations can make shared esteem that benefits the two investors and networks. This approach addresses a takeoff from the conventional view that organizations exist exclusively to produce benefits, stressing a more comprehensive and maintainable model of free enterprise.

At the core of shared esteem is the acknowledgment that social and financial advancement are associated. Organizations flourish in flourishing social orders, and cultural prosperity is dependent upon the mindful activities of organizations. This harmonious relationship challenges the division among benefit and reason, encouraging organizations to consider the more extensive effect of their choices on partners going from workers and clients to the climate and neighborhood networks.

Social business venture arises as a powerful power inside the convergence of business and social effect. Social business visionaries are people who influence business standards to address cultural difficulties, seeing business venture as a way to make positive and economical change. Their endeavors length many areas, from medical services and schooling to ecological preservation and neediness mitigation. What recognizes social business venture is the double obligation to monetary feasibility and social effect, showing the way that benefit and reason can coincide.

In the time of globalization, the elements of helpful and social effect are additionally impacted by the progression of data, merchandise, and thoughts across borders. While globalization has worked with extraordinary network and monetary development, it has additionally exposed the unmistakable disparities that endure inside and between countries. The bay between the well-off and the underestimated, both inside nations and on a worldwide scale, represents a significant test that requires aggregate and purposeful endeavors to connect.

Imbalances manifest in different structures, including financial variations, inconsistent admittance to schooling and medical care, and fundamental segregation in light of race, orientation, or financial status. Tending to these imbalances isn't just a question of civil rights yet in addition an essential for building a feasible and amicable worldwide society. Social effect drives that plan to change foundational imbalances frequently wrestle with the requirement for primary changes, strategy backing, and the development of comprehensive and various viewpoints.

The power elements intrinsic in philanthropic and social effect work highlight the significance of decolonizing ways to deal with improvement. By and large, mediations in underestimated networks have frequently been portrayed by paternalism and an absence of real organization. Decolonization in this setting includes destroying these power lopsided characteristics, focusing on nearby voices and office, and perceiving the inborn nobility and shrewdness inside networks.

The limitation of help and improvement endeavors is a vital guideline in decolonizing compassion. It accentuates the significance of drawing in with neighborhood networks as equivalent accomplices in the plan and execution of mediations. This approach perceives that networks have remarkable experiences into their own necessities and difficulties, and that supportable arrangements should be established in neighborhood settings. Besides, confinement adds to the strengthening of networks, encouraging a feeling of responsibility and organization in the improvement cycle.

The crossing point of philanthropy and social effect is maybe most apparent in the consequence of contentions and emergencies. Revamping social orders broke by brutality requires prompt help as well as a drawn out vision for supportable harmony and improvement. Temporary equity, a structure that looks to address the traditions of denials of basic liberties and advance compromise, turns into a pivotal part in post-struggle settings.

Momentary equity systems envelop a scope of intercessions, including truth and compromise commissions, indictments of culprits, repayments for casualties, and institutional changes. These drives point not exclusively to consider people responsible for past barbarities yet in addition to lay the foundation for an all the more and comprehensive society. The sensitive harmony among equity and compromise highlights the intricacies inborn in exploring the fallout of contention and highlights the requirement for setting explicit methodologies.

In struggle zones, kids frequently endure the worst part of brutality and uprooting, confronting prompt dangers to their security as well as long haul ramifications for their physical and mental prosperity. Schooling arises as a basic instrument for breaking the pattern of viciousness and offering youngsters a pathway to a more promising time to come. Schooling in struggle zones faces various difficulties, including the obliteration of framework, relocation of educators and understudies, and the mental injury experienced by kids.

Guaranteeing admittance to quality schooling in struggle impacted regions requires imaginative and setting explicit arrangements. Yet again innovation, ends up being an important partner in this undertaking. Remote learning drives, portable training applications, and local area based learning places are among the systems utilized to give instructive open doors to youngsters residing in the shadow of contention. Besides, instruction fills in as a vehicle for advancing resistance, understanding, and social attachment, establishing the groundwork for a more serene and strong society.

The nexus among philanthropy and social effect is likewise clear in the domain of general wellbeing. Worldwide wellbeing emergencies, like the Coronavirus pandemic, highlight the interconnectedness of human wellbeing and the requirement for facilitated global reactions. The pandemic has revealed existing wellbeing disparities, with minimized networks excessively impacted by the infection. Immunization crusades, general wellbeing framework, and evenhanded admittance to medical services arise as basic parts in the aggregate work to moderate the effect of the pandemic.

The job of local area wellbeing laborers becomes foremost in tending to wellbeing differences, especially in asset compelled settings. These bleeding edge laborers assume an essential part in conveying medical care administrations, advancing preventive measures, and overcoming any barrier among networks and formal wellbeing frameworks. Their work epitomizes the rule that manageable and successful wellbeing mediations should be established in local area commitment and customized to nearby settings.

Psychological wellness, long minimized in the talk on worldwide wellbeing, arises as a focal part of compassionate and social effect endeavors. The mental cost of emergencies, whether cataclysmic events, clashes, or pandemics, is significant and persevering. Shame encompassing psychological well-being further fuels the difficulties looked by people looking for help. Coordinating psychological wellness into philanthropic and social effect drives requires destigmatizing psychological wellness issues as well as building strong and socially touchy psychological well-being emotionally supportive networks.

As we explore the complicated scene of compassionate and social effect, the job of initiative turns into a point of convergence. Pioneers in these fields should have a blend of vision, compassion, and vital discernment to explore the unpredictable trap of difficulties. Administration isn't bound to progressive designs; it can arise at different levels, from grassroots local area pioneers to worldwide policymakers. Powerful forerunners in philanthropic and social effect work epitomize a promise to moral standards, a readiness to team up, and a comprehension of the nuanced settings in which they work.

All in all, the crossing point of philanthropy and social effect addresses a dynamic and developing scene. As we defy the difficulties of the present and future, a comprehensive and incorporated approach is fundamental.

Philanthropic endeavors, with their accentuation on quick help and empathy, should be supplemented by friendly effect drives that address the main drivers of human affliction and add to the drawn out prosperity of networks.

The interconnectedness of our worldwide local area requests joint effort, sympathy, and a common obligation to equity and fairness. Whether answering cataclysmic events, upholding for orientation balance, or revamping social orders torn by struggle, the quest for philanthropic and social effect requires aggregate activity. It requires an acknowledgment that, in the embroidery of our common humankind, each string is entwined with the others, making a texture that is versatile, merciful, and equipped for encouraging positive change on a worldwide scale.

7.1 Investigating the humanitarian and social challenges faced by the people of Jerusalem.

The city of Jerusalem remains as an image of verifiable importance, strict variety, and international intricacy. Settled in the core of the Center East, it is where the over a significant time span cross, and where the predeterminations of various networks are entwined. In the midst of its rich embroidery of social and strict legacy, individuals of Jerusalem wrestle with a bunch of helpful and social difficulties that mirror the intricacies of the district.

One of the essential difficulties confronting individuals of Jerusalem is the getting through Israeli-Palestinian clash, an extended battle an over area, personality, and sway. The city, venerated by Jews, Christians, and

Muslims, is a point of convergence of conflict, with the two Israelis and Palestinians guaranteeing it as their capital. The international pressures encompassing Jerusalem have expansive ramifications for the day to day routines of its inhabitants, affecting admittance to assets, opportunity of development, and the general strength of the district.

The issue of admittance to sacred locales is a focal part of the Israeli-Palestinian struggle in Jerusalem. The city is home to the absolute most respected strict locales on the planet, including the Western Wall, the Congregation of the Sacred Catacomb, and the Al-Aqsa Mosque. Admittance to these locales isn't just an issue of strict importance yet in addition a flashpoint for political strains. Limitations on access or episodes encompassing these sacred places frequently heighten pressures and add to an environment of question and hostility among various strict networks.

Notwithstanding the international difficulties, the financial differences inside Jerusalem present a critical helpful concern. The city is set apart by obvious imbalances between East Jerusalem, overwhelmingly Palestinian, and West Jerusalem, basically Jewish. East Jerusalem faces financial minimization, insufficient framework, and restricted admittance to fundamental administrations like training and medical services. The variations reflect more extensive financial difficulties looked by minimized networks, intensifying existing pressures and adding to a feeling of disappointment.

The issue of residency and character further entangles the social scene of Jerusalem. Palestinians in East Jerusalem, in spite of being occupants, face difficulties in getting Israeli citizenship, prompting a status portrayed by legitimate vagueness. This absence of clearness has suggestions for different parts of life, including business open doors, admittance to social administrations, and the capacity to unreservedly travel. The smoothness and vulnerability encompassing residency status add to a feeling of weakness and frailty among Palestinian inhabitants.

The development and extension of Israeli settlements in East Jerusalem present one more layer of intricacy to the philanthropic and social difficulties looked by the city's occupants. The development of settlements, thought about unlawful under global regulation, changes the segment organization of Jerusalem as well as disturbs the social texture of Palestinian people group. The development of settlements frequently prompts the uprooting of Palestinian families, making a pattern of dispossession and adding to the cracking of networks.

The instructive scene in Jerusalem mirrors the more extensive difficulties looked by the city. Instructive establishments in East Jerusalem frequently wrestle with restricted assets, packed study halls, and deficient framework. The variations in instructive open doors among East and West Jerusalem add to a pattern of disparity, restricting the possibilities for the more youthful age. Additionally, the school system isn't invulnerable to the more extensive political pressures, with educational programs and course books reflecting various stories, further developing splits between understudies.

Medical care is one more basic part of the helpful difficulties in Jerusalem. The variations in admittance to medical care administrations among East and West Jerusalem add to critical wellbeing imbalances. Palestinian occupants of East Jerusalem frequently face boundaries in getting to clinical offices, and the general wellbeing framework in the eastern area of the city is immature contrasted with the western part. This unevenness in medical care assets has significant ramifications for the prosperity of the populace, especially in the midst of emergencies like the Coronavirus pandemic.

The unpredictable snare of difficulties in Jerusalem stretches out to issues of water and asset circulation. Admittance to water is a central basic freedom, yet in Jerusalem, the circulation of water assets is a wellspring of conflict. Palestinian areas frequently experience water deficiencies and deficient framework, while Israeli settlements in East Jerusalem appreciate better admittance to water. The variations in asset designation add to a feeling of foul play and further strain relations between networks.

Social attachment and between local area relations in Jerusalem are profoundly impacted by the all-encompassing political setting. The presence of actual boundaries, like designated spots and the partition boundary, adds to a feeling of division and detachment among networks.

These boundaries influence day to day existence, limiting development, and making a tangible feeling of partition between various areas. The subsequent social fracture frustrates valuable open doors for discourse and common comprehension, propagating a pattern of doubt and ill will.

The mental cost of living in a city set apart by struggle and vulnerability is an unavoidable part of the philanthropic difficulties in Jerusalem. The consistent openness to political strains, safety efforts, and the flightiness of the circumstance adds to elevated feelings of anxiety among the occupants. Youngsters, specifically, endure the worst part of the mental effect, with encounters of injury, tension, and an upset feeling of predictability molding their early stages.

The media scene in Jerusalem assumes an essential part in forming discernments and stories, impacting popular assessment both locally and globally. The depiction of occasions, the outlining of issues, and the portrayal of various networks in the media add to the more extensive elements of the contention. Journalistic spin, falsehood, and the particular detailing of occurrences further muddle endeavors to encourage understanding and sympathy among various networks.

Common society drives in Jerusalem assume a crucial part in moderating the philanthropic and social difficulties looked by individuals of the city. Non-legislative associations (NGOs), people group based associations, and grassroots developments work indefatigably to address the prompt requirements of weak populaces, advance discourse, and backer for strategy changes. These drives work in testing conditions, exploring political responsive qualities and asset limitations to have an unmistakable effect on the ground.

The job of global entertainers in tending to the difficulties of Jerusalem couldn't possibly be more significant. The global local area, through conciliatory channels, philanthropic help, and improvement projects, assumes a significant part in impacting the direction of occasions in the city. Worldwide associations, including the Assembled Countries, work to offer fundamental types of assistance, advocate for basic freedoms, and work with exchange between clashing gatherings. In any case, the viability of global mediations is much of the time blocked by international intricacies and the absence of an extensive and comprehensive harmony process.

Endeavors to address the philanthropic and social difficulties in Jerusalem should focus on a thorough and comprehensive methodology. A fair and enduring goal to the Israeli-Palestinian struggle is fundamental for making the circumstances essential for practical turn of events and social union in the city. Such a goal ought to include issues of lines, exiles, the situation with Jerusalem, and the acknowledgment of the privileges and desires of the two Israelis and Palestinians.

Interfaith discourse and drives that advance social trade are vital parts of building spans between various networks in Jerusalem. Perceiving the common legacy of the city and cultivating shared regard among its different occupants are fundamental stages toward making a more comprehensive and amicable social texture. Strict pioneers, local area activists, and teachers can assume vital parts in advancing resilience and understanding.

Putting resources into the improvement of East Jerusalem is a vital component in tending to financial variations and cultivating a feeling of value among the city's occupants. This incorporates further developing framework, extending admittance to quality instruction and medical services, and setting out monetary open doors that benefit all networks. Manageable improvement projects, directed by standards of inclusivity and participatory navigation, can add to building a stronger and interconnected city.

The strengthening of ladies in Jerusalem is a cross-cutting technique for tending to social difficulties. Ladies, frequently at the very front of local area flexibility, can assume critical parts in advancing discourse, supporting for civil rights, and cultivating financial turn of events. Drives that enable ladies financially, socially, and politically contribute not exclusively to orientation uniformity yet in addition to the general prosperity of networks.

Global entertainers ought to focus on drives that help neighborhood common society associations chipping away at the ground. These associations, with their cozy information on nearby elements, are strategically set up to address the prompt requirements of weak populaces and backer for long haul foundational change. Worldwide help ought to be lined up with the standards of inclusivity, regarding the organization of nearby entertainers and intensifying their endeavors.

Training arises as a key part in the more extensive procedure to address the difficulties of Jerusalem. Comprehensive and evenhanded instruction that advances decisive reasoning, intercultural understanding, and compromise abilities can add to breaking the pattern of question and enmity. Additionally, instructive drives ought to be intended to encourage a feeling of divided citizenship and having a place between the city's different populace.

Tending to the compassionate and social difficulties of Jerusalem requires supported responsibility, versatility, and an acknowledgment of the interconnectedness of various issues. While the political components of the Israeli-Palestinian clash stay complicated, the emphasis on the human aspect — the desires, needs, and freedoms of individuals of Jerusalem — can direct endeavors toward an additional equitable and economical future. It is in the common quest for respect, equity, and a superior life for all that the genuine capability of Jerusalem as a city of harmony can be understood.

7.2 Highlighting initiatives and organizations working towards social justice and human rights.

In the broad scene of civil rights and basic liberties, a horde of drives and associations stand as encouraging signs, working vigorously to address foundational disparities, safeguard central opportunities, and promoter for the freedoms of minimized networks. These undertakings length the globe, mirroring a common obligation to building an additional impartial and simply world. This investigation digs into the multi-layered domain of civil rights and basic liberties drives, focusing on the groundbreaking work being embraced by different associations.

At the front of the worldwide common liberties development is Reprieve Global, a spearheading association with a celebrated history of upholding for equity and nobility. Reprieve Global works on a rule of unprejudiced nature, shielding the freedoms of people independent of political affiliations, race, or doctrine. Through thorough examination, promotion, and missions, Reprieve Worldwide addresses a wide range of common liberties issues, from political constraint and segregation to the situation of evacuees and capital punishment.

Basic liberties Watch, one more sturdy in the common freedoms scene, conducts fastidious examinations and uncovered mishandles around the world. With an emphasis on considering states and strong entertainers responsible for their activities, Basic freedoms Watch plays had a critical impact in enhancing the voices of those confronting mistreatment. Its reports and support endeavors add to molding worldwide strategies and cultivating a culture of responsibility for basic freedoms infringement.

Nearer to home, the American Common Freedoms Association (ACLU) has been a rampart in shielding common freedoms in the US. Established in 1920, the ACLU has a rich tradition of guarding sacred privileges, including the right to speak freely of discourse, the right to security, and equivalent assurance under the law. Through case, promotion, and state funded training, the ACLU has been instrumental in forming legitimate points of reference that safeguard the privileges of people against bureaucratic power grabbing.

In the domain of orientation equity and ladies' privileges, UN Ladies arises as a worldwide power for groundbreaking change. As the Assembled Countries substance committed to orientation correspondence, UN Ladies attempts to dispense with segregation and viciousness against ladies, advance financial strengthening, and guarantee ladies' cooperation in dynamic cycles. Its drives range from grassroots local area undertakings to significant level backing for strategy changes on the worldwide stage.

On the African mainland, the Legitimate Assets Place (LRC) in South Africa epitomizes the crossing point of lawful backing and civil rights. Laid out during the politically-sanctioned racial segregation period, the LRC assumed a critical part in involving the law as a device for social change. Its work stretches out to issues, for example, land privileges, admittance to instruction, and ecological equity, mirroring a promise to tending to verifiable and contemporary treacheries.

In India, the Mazdoor Kisan Shakti Sangathan (MKSS) remains as a grassroots development upholding for the privileges of laborers and ranchers. Established in the mid 1990s, MKSS spearheaded the utilization of Right to Data (RTI) regulations to battle debasement and guarantee straightforwardness in administration. Its activation endeavors have enabled minimized networks to request their privileges and challenge fundamental treacheries.

In the computerized age, the Electronic Boondocks Establishment (EFF) assumes a critical part in shielding common freedoms in the domain of innovation. With an emphasis on safeguarding security, free articulation, and development, the EFF participates in legitimate backing, strategy examination, and grassroots activism. In a period where innovation converges with each part of our lives, the EFF's work is vital to guaranteeing that progressions in the computerized domain don't think twice about basic freedoms.

The battle for LGBTQ+ freedoms finds a strong backer in the Common liberties Mission (HRC) in the US. Attempting to guarantee that each individual can live liberated from separation paying little heed to sexual direction or orientation character, the HRC takes part in regulative promotion, government funded schooling, and corporate effort. Its endeavors have added to critical headways in LGBTQ+ freedoms, including marriage uniformity and against segregation assurances.

The battle against racial unfairness is exemplified by associations like the NAACP (Public Relationship for the Headway of Minorities Individuals) in the US. Established in 1909, the NAACP has been a vigorous backer for the freedoms of African Americans, battling fundamental prejudice through legitimate activity, grassroots getting sorted out, and public mindfulness crusades. The association's heritage remembers milestone triumphs for the battle for social liberties.

At the nexus of ecological equity and basic liberties, Greenpeace remains as a worldwide power for promotion and direct activity. With a mission to safeguard the planet and advance harmony, Greenpeace crusades against ecological debasement, environmental change, and corporate practices that undermine biological systems and human prosperity. Its striking and frequently trying activities catch worldwide consideration and catalyze public talk on ecological issues.

Directing concentration toward the domain of monetary equity, Oxfam Worldwide works as a confederation of associations focused on tending to destitution and imbalance. Through improvement projects, promotion, and exploration, Oxfam handles issues, for example, fair work rehearses, admittance to training, and abundance imbalance. The association's yearly reports on worldwide abundance conveyance feature the unmistakable variations that persevere on the planet, starting discussions on the requirement for foundational change.

The Worldwide Work Association (ILO), a particular organization of the Unified Countries, centers around advancing civil rights and work privileges internationally. Laid out in 1919, the ILO sets global work guidelines and attempts to guarantee respectable working circumstances, fair wages, and social assurance for laborers. Its three sided structure, uniting states, managers, and laborers, mirrors a cooperative way to deal with tending to work issues.

With regards to relocation and displaced person freedoms, the Global Association for Movement (IOM) assumes a basic part in tending to the difficulties looked by transients around the world. With an emphasis on advancing sympathetic and methodical relocation, the IOM offers fundamental types of assistance, advocates for traveler freedoms, and adds to strategy improvement at the public and global levels. Its work includes both emergency reaction and long haul answers for transients and uprooted populaces.

The Worldwide Asset to Battle Helps, Tuberculosis, and Jungle fever represents the convergence of wellbeing and common liberties. Laid out as an organization between states, common society, and the confidential area, the Worldwide Asset prepares assets to battle three of the world's most wrecking illnesses. Its methodology perceives that wellbeing isn't just a clinical issue yet in addition an essential common freedom, requiring a complete and comprehensive reaction.

In the domain of native freedoms, Social Endurance remains as an association devoted to safeguarding the privileges of native people groups all over the planet. Through promotion, exploration, and media drives, Social Endurance attempts to engage native networks, save their social legacy, and safeguard their property privileges. The association's accentuation on intensifying native voices guarantees that their points of view and battles are at the very front of the basic freedoms talk.

Chasing enhancement in law enforcement, Guiltlessness Task plays had a vital impact in excusing illegitimately sentenced people through DNA testing. Established in 1992, the Honesty Undertaking uses lawful backing, state funded schooling, and strategy drives to address blemishes in the law enforcement framework. Its work features the critical requirement for fundamental changes to forestall unsuccessful labors of equity and guarantee a fair and impartial lawful interaction.

On the worldwide stage, the Assembled Countries High Magistrate for Common freedoms (OHCHR) fills in as a chief promoter for basic liberties inside the UN framework. The High Chief and the OHCHR work to advance and safeguard common liberties around the world, leading examinations, checking basic freedoms circumstances, and offering help to nations in building strong basic freedoms establishments. The OHCHR assumes a vital part in propelling the global basic liberties plan and considering states responsible for their responsibilities.

In the circle of schooling and youth strengthening, Malala Asset stands apart as an association focused on guaranteeing that each young lady approaches 12 years of free, safe, and quality training. Named after Nobel laureate Malala Yousafzai, the Malala Asset advocates for strategy changes, puts resources into nearby schooling undertakings, and enhances the voices of young ladies upholding for their right to training. Its work rises above public lines, tending to the worldwide test of guaranteeing instructive open doors for all.

Neighborhood drives likewise assume a urgent part in the embroidery of civil rights endeavors. The Destitute Pre-birth Program in San Francisco, for instance, centers around breaking the pattern of young life neediness by offering help and assets to families encountering vagrancy. Through a comprehensive methodology that incorporates lodging help, medical services, and training, the program engages families to defeat the difficulties of vagrancy and construct a steady future.

The Middle for Established Freedoms (CCR) in the US is a lawful support association that uses case and legitimate methodologies to propel civil rights purposes. From provoking biased strategies to addressing survivors of denials of basic freedoms, the CCR works at the crossing point of regulation and activism. Its milestone cases have had sweeping ramifications for common freedoms and basic liberties insurances.

With regards to LGBTQ+ privileges support, the Trevor Undertaking has been a pioneer in giving emergency mediation and self destruction counteraction administrations for LGBTQ+ youth. Through its helpline, online assets, and promotion drives, the Trevor Venture tends to the extraordinary difficulties looked by LGBTQ+ people, making a steady and confirming space for those out of luck. Its work adds to more extensive endeavors to battle segregation and advance inclusivity.

Chasing inability privileges, the World Organization on Incapacity (WID) attempts to dispose of boundaries and engage individuals with handicaps universally. Through research, strategy promotion, and limit building, WID resolves issues like availability, comprehensive schooling, and the freedoms of individuals with inabilities to autonomously live. Endeavors add to molding strategies and practices advance the full cooperation of people with handicaps in the public eye.

The interconnectedness of common freedoms issues is clear in crafted by associations like Worldwide Observer, which centers around uncovering and testing the connections between regular asset double-dealing, struggle, and denials of basic liberties. Through examinations and backing, Worldwide Observer reveals insight into debasement, ecological corruption, and savagery related with the extraction of normal assets. Its work highlights the basic of tending to the underlying drivers of common freedoms infringement chasing after equity.

As the worldwide local area faces the earnest test of environmental change, developments like Fridays for Future, drove by youth lobbyist Greta Thunberg, have arisen as strong backers for ecological equity. Through school strikes and public mindfulness crusades, Fridays for Future activates youngsters all over the planet to request activity on environmental change. The development represents the capability of grassroots drives to drive foundational change and consider state run administrations responsible for their natural arrangements.

In the domain of work privileges, the Fair Food Program in the US tends to double-dealing and maltreatment inside the agrarian business. Through an organization between farmworkers, producers, and retail food organizations, the Fair Food Program guarantees fair wages, empathetic working circumstances, and components for tending to work infringement. Its creative model exhibits that extraordinary change is conceivable through cooperation and a promise to common freedoms.

The above models address simply a small portion of the huge scene of drives and associations devoted to civil rights and basic freedoms. Their work traverses assorted issues, districts, and networks, mirroring the comprehensiveness of the battle for equity and respect. These drives show that groundbreaking change is conceivable through a mix of legitimate promotion, grassroots preparation, strategy changes, and worldwide participation.

Nonetheless, the difficulties are imposing, and the work is not even close to finish. The determination of fundamental imbalances, separation, and denials of basic liberties requires a continuous and aggregate obligation to address main drivers and make enduring arrangements. The multifacetedness of civil rights issues requests all encompassing methodologies that perceive the interconnected idea of various battles and focus on the voices and organization of impacted networks.

7.3 Discussing the global implications of addressing these issues in Jerusalem.

Tending to the complicated trap of social, helpful, and policy centered issues in Jerusalem resounds a long ways past the city's old walls. The worldwide ramifications of handling these difficulties stretch out into the domains of discretion, peacebuilding, common freedoms support, and the more extensive quest for global security. Jerusalem, with its verifiable, strict, and international importance, fills in as a microcosm of more extensive worldwide elements, making the goal of its issues significant for encouraging an additional fair and impartial world.

The Israeli-Palestinian struggle, at the core of many difficulties in Jerusalem, has for quite some time been a point of convergence of global concern. The goal of this contention is viewed as essential to accomplishing provincial strength and worldwide harmony. The interconnectedness of the Center East with worldwide energy assets, shipping lanes, and security contemplations implies that the gradually expanding influences of contention in Jerusalem are felt on a worldwide scale.

Tending to the underlying drivers of the contention and pursuing an equitable and enduring arrangement holds the possibility to add to more extensive endeavors for harmony in the locale.

The situation with Jerusalem itself is a profoundly touchy and universally challenged issue. The city's importance to Judaism, Christianity, and Islam makes it a point of convergence for strict pressures, with suggestions past the prompt locale. A goal that regards the strict privileges and responsive qualities of all networks in Jerusalem could start a trend for tending to comparable difficulties in different districts where strict contrasts add to struggle.

The financial variations inside Jerusalem, especially among East and West Jerusalem, reflect worldwide examples of imbalance. The glaring difference in everyday environments, admittance to assets, and open doors for occupants of various pieces of the city mirrors a more extensive worldwide pattern of financial variations among wealthy and underestimated networks. Tending to these financial difficulties in Jerusalem could add to a more extensive discussion on the requirement for comprehensive monetary turn of events and civil rights around the world.

The development and extension of settlements in East Jerusalem are seen by the worldwide local area as an infringement of global regulation. The ramifications of such settlements stretch out past the Israeli-Palestinian setting, resounding with worldwide discussions on regional honesty, power, and the privileges of native populaces. The worldwide local area's reaction to settlement development in Jerusalem starts a trend for how such issues are tended to in different districts wrestling with inquiries of land privileges and regional questions.

The right to instruction, a crucial basic freedom frequently impeded by struggle, is a worldwide concern. In Jerusalem, the difficulties looked by Palestinian understudies in getting to quality schooling because of limitations, asset differences, and the effect of the contention reflect snags experienced by minimized populaces in other struggle zones all over the planet. The worldwide local area's obligation to guaranteeing training for everything is reflected in its reaction to challenges looked by understudies in Jerusalem.

Medical services access, a basic part of human prosperity, is likewise profoundly impacted by the difficulties in Jerusalem. The variations in medical care assets among East and West Jerusalem reverberation worldwide wellbeing imbalances where underestimated networks face restricted admittance to fundamental administrations. The Coronavirus pandemic has highlighted the interconnectedness of worldwide wellbeing, accentuating the significance of fair medical services frameworks to guarantee the prosperity of people all over.

The mental cost of living in a city set apart by struggle, vulnerability, and political pressure is a common involvement in populaces in other clash zones. Psychological well-being difficulties coming about because of openness to brutality, dislodging, and uncertainty are general worries that request worldwide consideration.

Tending to the psychological wellness effect of contention in Jerusalem could add to a more extensive comprehension of the significance of emotional well-being support in helpful and struggle settings universally.

The media's part in forming stories and discernments is a worldwide peculiarity, and the elements in Jerusalem reverberation more extensive worries about journalistic spin, deception, and the impact of media on general assessment. The worldwide local area's commitment with media-related difficulties in Jerusalem mirrors an acknowledgment of the significance of media education, dependable news coverage, and the job of data in molding stories in different worldwide settings.

The outcast emergency, an outcome of contention and relocation in Jerusalem, reverberates with the more extensive worldwide exile challenge. The predicament of evacuees in Jerusalem and the requirement for economical arrangements equal the battles looked by uprooted populaces around the world. The worldwide local area's reaction to the evacuee emergency in Jerusalem starts trends for tending to comparable difficulties in different districts, stressing the requirement for exhaustive and privileges based ways to deal with dislodging.

The standards of decolonization in compassionate endeavors, exemplified by the significance of drawing in with nearby networks as equivalent accomplices in the advancement cycle, have importance past Jerusalem. The call for destroying power awkward nature, perceiving neighborhood office, and cultivating comprehensive improvement models addresses the requirement for additional fair and participatory ways to deal with philanthropic and advancement work around the world.

The convergence of compassion and social effect, clear in endeavors to address the main drivers of human affliction and advance long haul prosperity in Jerusalem, offers experiences for worldwide philanthropic and improvement techniques. The accentuation on economical arrangements, local area drove improvement, and an all encompassing way to deal with tending to emergencies gives a model to viable and significant mediations in different districts wrestling with complex difficulties.

The interconnectedness of worldwide difficulties and the basic of global participation are apparent in the Assembled Countries' job in tending to the helpful and social difficulties in Jerusalem. The Unified Countries, with its obligation to the Economical Improvement Objectives (SDGs) and standards of value and equity, mirrors a more extensive affirmation that worldwide issues require aggregate and facilitated reactions.

Corporate social obligation (CSR), as exemplified by innovation organizations engaged with drives to give instructive open doors and backing emotional well-being administrations in Jerusalem, mirrors a more extensive pattern of organizations perceiving their part in friendly effect.

The commitment of the confidential area in tending to cultural difficulties lines up with worldwide conversations on the job of organizations in adding to social great and economical turn of events.

8

Chapter 8

Technological and Innovation Hub

The idea of a Mechanical and Development Center point has acquired critical conspicuousness as of late as social orders all over the planet progressively perceive the crucial job that innovation and development play in driving monetary development, cultivating cultural advancement, and tending to worldwide difficulties. A Mechanical and Development Center fills in as a point of convergence for the combination of state of the art advancements, innovative work exercises, pioneering tries, and cooperative drives. This exhaustive environment is intended to catalyze development, support ability, and speed up the speed of mechanical headway.

At the core of a Mechanical and Development Center point lies a pledge to establishing a climate that cultivates innovativeness, coordinated effort, and the consistent reconciliation of different disciplines. These center points are in many cases decisively situated in metropolitan places or assigned advancement regions, where they can use existing foundation, scholarly establishments, and industry groups. The objective is to make a unique biological system that draws in a different scope of partners, including scientists, business people, financial backers, and industry pioneers, encouraging a lively and interconnected local area.

One of the critical highlights of a Mechanical and Development Center is its accentuation on interdisciplinary cooperation. By separating customary storehouses and empowering cross-disciplinary connections, these center points make a ripe ground for the intermingling of thoughts from different fields. This interdisciplinary methodology is fundamental for handling complex difficulties that require assorted points of view and mastery. In a Mechanical and Development Center, specialists from various disciplines can team up on projects that push the limits of information and lead to weighty advancements.

Training and expertise improvement are indispensable parts of a Mechanical and Development Center point. Perceiving that a knowledgeable and gifted labor force is basic for driving innovative advancement, these center points frequently house instructive foundations, preparing focuses, and research offices. By giving admittance to quality schooling and preparing programs, these center points mean to develop a pool of ability outfitted with the abilities and information required for the positions representing things to come.

Moreover, a Mechanical and Development Center fills in as a magnet for both homegrown and worldwide ability. The worldwide idea of development implies that the best personalities might be dissipated across the world. These center points establish a climate that draws in top ability by offering best in class offices, admittance to state of the art research valuable open doors, and a cooperative environment that cultivates nonstop learning.

Notwithstanding instruction, one more key mainstay of a Mechanical and Development Center is business. These centers effectively support the creation and development of new businesses by giving brooding spaces, mentorship programs, admittance to subsidizing, and organizing amazing open doors. By supporting a lively startup environment, these center points add to work creation, financial broadening, and the improvement of a culture that values risk-taking and development.

Government support and key organizations assume a vital part in the progress of a Mechanical and Development Center. Legislatures frequently give monetary motivations, administrative help, and framework improvement to catalyze the development of these centers. Also, producing associations with industry pioneers, research foundations, and global associations upgrades the center point's abilities and expands its scope.

The approach of arising advances, like man-made consciousness, blockchain, and high level assembling, has additionally uplifted the significance of Mechanical and Development Centers. These center points become proving grounds for the commonsense utilization of new advances, permitting scientists and organizations to investigate their likely effect on different businesses. The fast speed of mechanical change likewise requires constant transformation, causing these center points dynamic focuses that to develop with the moving innovative scene.

The effect of a fruitful Mechanical and Development Center stretches out past financial contemplations. These centers add to the making of an information based economy, where development turns into a main impetus for feasible turn of events. Besides, by encouraging a culture of interest and request, these centers add to a general public that values learning and embraces change.

A Mechanical and Development Center point isn't restricted to a particular industry or area. All things being equal, it incorporates a wide range of disciplines, going from data innovation and biotechnology to sustainable power and high level materials. This variety guarantees that the center point stays strong to financial vacillations and can adjust to arising patterns.

In the domain of innovative work, a Mechanical and Development Center point fills in as a core for spearheading revelations and forward leaps. Research foundations inside the center point team up on projects that push the limits of information, investigating unknown domains and looking for answers for a portion of the world's most squeezing difficulties. The cooperative idea of these centers empowers scientists to use each other's skill, share assets, and speed up the speed of revelation.

Besides, a Mechanical and Advancement Center gives a stage to the improvement of evidence of-idea models and pilot projects. This is especially vital in ventures where unmistakable models are fundamental for drawing in speculation and testing the reasonability of new advances. By giving the fundamental framework and backing, these center points work with the change from conceptualization to execution.

The union of the scholarly world and industry is a sign of effective Mechanical and Development Center points. Scholarly organizations inside the center point team up intimately with industry accomplices to guarantee that examination results are lined up with certifiable necessities. This industry-the scholarly community collaboration upgrades the pertinence of exploration as well as works with the commercialization of developments, making a consistent pathway from the research facility to the commercial center.

With regards to computerized change, a Mechanical and Development Center point assumes a crucial part in driving the reception of cutting edge innovations by organizations. Organizations inside the center point have the valuable chance to team up with innovation specialists, access state of the art research, and partake in pilot projects that show the useful utilizations of arising advances. This involved experience speeds up the reception bend and positions organizations inside the center point as early adopters and trend-setters in their particular enterprises.

Moreover, the presence of a Mechanical and Development Center improves the worldwide seriousness of the locale. As development turns into a vital driver of monetary achievement, districts that secure themselves as centers for mechanical headway draw in speculation, ability, and organizations from around the world.

This worldwide interconnectedness cultivates a feeling of solid rivalry and coordinated effort, with center points competing to be at the front line of the following flood of mechanical development.

The progress of a Mechanical and Development Center point relies on its capacity to make a strong biological system that supports innovativeness and hazard taking. This requires a mix of actual foundation, administrative structures, and social factors that all in all add to a favorable climate for development. The actual framework incorporates cutting edge research offices, cooperative work areas, and hatching focuses. Administrative structures ought to be spry and steady, cultivating advancement while guaranteeing moral and capable practices. Socially, the center point ought to advance a mentality that embraces disappointment as a learning an open door, values variety of thought, and celebrates achievement.

Open development is a key rule supporting the working of a Mechanical and Advancement Center point. This includes effectively looking for outer thoughts, cooperation, and associations to supplement inward capacities. By drawing in with a different organization of supporters, including new companies, research establishments, and industry accomplices, the center point can take advantage of a more extensive pool of information and assets. Open development speeds up the speed of advancement as well as cultivates a culture of coordinated effort and information sharing.

The job of subsidizing in the outcome of a Mechanical and Development Center point couldn't possibly be more significant. Monetary help is fundamental for supporting examination exercises, giving seed financing to new businesses, and redesigning framework to stay up with mechanical headways. State run administrations, confidential financial backers, and generous associations all assume vital parts in giving the fundamental subsidizing to guarantee the drawn out suitability of the center point.

Coordinated effort on a worldwide scale is one more key part of a Mechanical and Development Center point. Worldwide difficulties, for example, environmental change, medical services emergencies, and network safety dangers, require cooperative arrangements that rise above public limits. By cultivating global associations, these center points make an organization of skill that can all in all address difficulties that no single element or nation can handle alone. Also, worldwide cooperation upgrades the worldwide perceivability of the center point, drawing in ability and venture from around the world.

The idea of a Mechanical and Development Center isn't bound to created economies. Non-industrial nations likewise perceive the groundbreaking capability of innovation and advancement in jumping customary improvement pathways. Laying out centers in creating areas can catalyze financial development, make occupations, and address neighborhood challenges through imaginative arrangements.

In any case, the outcome of such center points in creating settings requires an essential methodology that thinks about neighborhood subtleties, puts resources into training and expertise improvement, and use native information and assets.

The moral contemplations related with mechanical progressions can't be neglected in that frame of mind of an Innovative and Development Center point. As innovation develops, moral inquiries connected with protection, security, inclination, and the effect on society become progressively mind boggling. Center points must proactively address these moral worries by integrating moral systems into innovative work processes, advancing straightforwardness, and taking part in discourse with partners to guarantee mindful development.

The continuous development of a Mechanical and Development Center is intently attached to its capacity to expect and adjust to arising patterns. Innovations, for example, quantum registering, high level mechanical technology, and quality altering are ready to reclassify enterprises and make additional opportunities. Center points that stay at the front of these turns of events, putting resources into research and establishing a climate that energizes trial and error, will keep on being center points of development in the years to come.

All in all, a Mechanical and Development Center addresses a change in perspective in the manner social orders approach financial turn of events and progress. By making dynamic biological systems that cultivate cooperation, instruction, business, and exploration, these centers become focal points of development with sweeping effects. The fruitful foundation and development of a Mechanical and Development Center require a comprehensive methodology that incorporates actual framework, administrative help, monetary speculation, and a culture that values innovativeness and versatility. As the world explores the difficulties and chances of the computerized age, these centers arise as encouraging signs, driving positive change and forming a future where development is at the very front of cultural headway.

8.1 Exploring Jerusalem's role as a center for innovation and technology.

Jerusalem, loved by three significant monotheistic religions, isn't just a city of verifiable and social importance yet is progressively arising as a middle for development and innovation. While its old roads give testimony regarding centuries of mankind's set of experiences, the cutting edge horizon is becoming dabbed with center points of innovative progression, new companies, and exploration foundations. This extraordinary juxtaposition of custom and development positions Jerusalem as an enamoring contextual analysis in how a city well established in history can likewise embrace the future through mechanical advancement.

At the core of Jerusalem's developing standing as a middle for development is its flourishing startup biological system. Customarily known for its strict and social legacy, the city has effectively broadened its financial scene by cultivating a helpful climate for new businesses and innovation organizations.

Hatcheries, gas pedals, and collaborating spaces have become fundamental parts of Jerusalem's innovative biological system, giving a steady framework to sprouting business visionaries to transform their thoughts into the real world.

A few variables add to Jerusalem's allure for new companies. First and foremost, the city benefits from a rich pool of ability, including moves on from its eminent scholarly organizations. Establishments, for example, the Jewish College of Jerusalem and the Technion-Israel Foundation of Innovation are centers of state of the art research, creating graduates with the abilities and information expected in the advanced tech scene. The nearness of these scholarly foundations to the startup environment works with consistent cooperation among the scholarly world and industry.

Besides, Jerusalem's different populace, addressing a mosaic of societies and foundations, adds to an imaginative and dynamic air. The convergence of alternate points of view frequently prompts creative arrangements and a great many thoughts. This variety is an important resource in a period where development flourishes with the union of disciplines and the mixing of thoughts from different sources.

Government support plays had an essential impact in energizing Jerusalem's mechanical change. Perceiving the financial capability of a vigorous development area, the Israeli government has carried out strategies and drives to energize the development of new companies. Monetary motivating forces, awards, and tax reductions are among the devices used to invigorate development and draw in both homegrown and unfamiliar venture. Moreover, government organizations team up with private area partners to establish an administrative climate that works with business and mechanical turn of events.

Jerusalem's startup scene isn't restricted to a particular industry; it traverses many areas, including medical care, biotechnology, network protection, and man-made consciousness. The city's remarkable situation as a scaffold among East and West, alongside its verifiable importance, has added to the improvement of creative arrangements that address worldwide difficulties. For example, Jerusalem-based new businesses are effectively engaged with creating innovations to upgrade clinical medicines, work on rural practices, and reinforce network safety measures.

The medical care area, specifically, has seen huge advancement in Jerusalem. The city has clinical exploration communities and clinics that team up with new companies to spearhead progressions in clinical innovation. From customized medication to advanced wellbeing arrangements, Jerusalem's medical services environment is at the bleeding edge of tending to the developing requirements of the worldwide medical services industry. The cooperative energy between clinical examination foundations and enterprising endeavors has made a rich ground for forward leaps that can possibly influence lives around the world.

In the domain of biotechnology, Jerusalem's commitments are essential. The city is home to organizations participated in hereditary examination, drug revelation, and the improvement of imaginative treatments. The combination of biotechnology with different disciplines, like information science and man-made consciousness, is bringing about original methodologies in understanding and treating illnesses. Jerusalem's biotech new businesses are progressing logical information as well as adding to the interpretation of examination discoveries into pragmatic applications.

Online protection is another region where Jerusalem has taken critical steps. Given the rising recurrence and refinement of digital dangers all around the world, the interest for powerful network safety arrangements is higher than at any other time. Jerusalem-based network safety new companies influence the city's mechanical mastery to foster inventive answers for safeguarding delicate data and basic framework. The cooperative environment in Jerusalem permits these new companies to work intimately with government offices, guard associations, and global accomplices to address arising network safety challenges.

Man-made brainpower (artificial intelligence) and AI are indispensable parts of Jerusalem's innovative scene. The city's scholastic organizations are at the very front of man-made intelligence exploration, and new businesses are tackling this aptitude to foster computer based intelligence driven answers for different enterprises. Applications range from normal language handling and PC vision to prescient examination and independent frameworks. Jerusalem's computer based intelligence environment mirrors a pledge to utilizing state of the art innovations to drive development and address complex issues.

The union of custom and innovation is maybe most apparent in the domain of social legacy protection. Jerusalem's verifiable importance and social lavishness have prodded the advancement of imaginative innovations pointed toward safeguarding and advancing social legacy. From augmented reality encounters that reproduce authentic occasions to advanced files that protect antiquated original copies, innovation is being tackled to guarantee that the city's social heritage is open to people in the future.

Jerusalem's job as a middle for development reaches out past the bounds of its startup biological system. The city is likewise a center for innovative work, with scholastic establishments and examination focuses driving progressions in different fields. The Jewish College of Jerusalem, specifically, has a recognized history of scholastic greatness and examination commitments. Its coordinated efforts with industry accomplices and new companies add to the exchange of information from the scholarly circle to useful applications on the lookout.

Worldwide joint effort is a vital component of Jerusalem's development scene. The city's new businesses and research establishments effectively participate in associations with partners all over the planet.

These joint efforts work with the trading of thoughts, mastery, and assets, enhancing the neighborhood development environment and adding to worldwide progressions. Jerusalem's worldwide associations enhance its effect on the global stage, situating the city as a vital participant in the worldwide development scene.

Challenges, be that as it may, go with the potential open doors introduced by Jerusalem's excursion into the domain of innovation and advancement. The international setting in the district presents intricacies that can influence the progression of ability, speculation, and coordinated effort. Exploring these difficulties requires strength, strategy, and a guarantee to cultivating a comprehensive and cooperative climate that rises above international limits.

While Jerusalem's tech scene has accomplished huge achievements, there is an acknowledgment that supported development requires ceaseless interest in training and expertise improvement. Guaranteeing that the labor force is furnished with the abilities requested by the quickly developing tech scene is fundamental for the drawn out progress of the city's advancement biological system. Drives zeroed in on STEM (science, innovation, designing, and math) schooling, professional preparation, and long lasting learning are basic to supporting the ability pipeline.

The moral elements of mechanical development additionally come to the bleeding edge in Jerusalem, as in any tech center point. As progressions in regions like simulated intelligence, biotechnology, and network protection keep on reshaping businesses and social orders, moral contemplations become fundamental. Guaranteeing that advancement is directed by standards of reasonableness, straightforwardness, and social obligation is essential for building trust and relieving expected gambles.

8.2 Highlighting advancements in science, medicine, and technology originating from Jerusalem.

Jerusalem, with its rich embroidery of history and culture, has not exclusively been a support of progress however has likewise turned into a wellspring of momentous headways in science, medication, and innovation. The city's commitments range hundreds of years, and in the cutting edge time, it keeps on being a center point of development, pushing the limits of information and reshaping the scene of logical and mechanical advancement.

In the domain of science, Jerusalem has been a focal point of scholarly request and revelation since old times. The city's profound authentic roots have drawn in researchers and scholars, encouraging a climate helpful for logical investigation. This practice of request has persevered through the ages, with contemporary specialists expanding on the establishments laid by their ancestors.

One prominent area of logical progression beginning from Jerusalem is prehistoric studies. The city's archeological locales are mother lodes of authentic curios and experiences into antiquated civic establishments.

The careful work of archeologists in Jerusalem has uncovered layers of history, uncovering the design wonders, social practices, and cultural designs of former periods. These disclosures not just add to how we might interpret the past yet in addition give important examples to the present and future.

Jerusalem's academic local area has additionally taken critical steps in natural examination and reasonable practices. With a developing consciousness of the worldwide natural difficulties, scientists in the city are utilizing their skill to foster imaginative arrangements. From water protection innovations to sustainable power drives, Jerusalem's logical undertakings add to the worldwide work to resolve squeezing natural issues and make a practical future.

Medication, another circle where Jerusalem sparkles, has seen earth shattering headways beginning from the city's examination foundations and clinical focuses. The Jewish College of Jerusalem, as a team with Hadassah Clinical Center, has been at the cutting edge of clinical examination, spearheading improvements that influence medical services worldwide. Research in regions like immunology, oncology, and nervous system science has collected worldwide praise, putting Jerusalem on the guide as a center for clinical development.

Jerusalem's clinical examination stretches out to customized medication, where headways in genomics and atomic science are forming the fate of medical care. Fitting medicines in light of a person's hereditary cosmetics holds huge commitment for additional powerful and designated mediations. Jerusalem's specialists are effectively participated in disentangling the complexities of the human genome, prompting forward leaps that can possibly alter how we approach sickness anticipation and therapy.

Besides, the city plays had a significant impact in progressing regenerative medication and undifferentiated organism research. These fields hold the way to fixing and recovering harmed tissues, offering expect patients with degenerative illnesses and wounds. Jerusalem's academic local area, as a team with clinical professionals, is at the very front of creating regenerative treatments that could change the scene of medical services, giving new roads to recuperating and recuperation.

In the field of innovation, Jerusalem's impact is progressively conspicuous, especially in the fields of network protection and data innovation. With the ascent of advanced availability, the requirement for hearty network protection measures has become fundamental. Jerusalem-based organizations and exploration foundations are effectively taken part in creating imaginative online protection arrangements, tending to the advancing difficulties presented by digital dangers.

The city's aptitude in data innovation reaches out to programming advancement, computerized reasoning, and information examination. Jerusalem-based new businesses and tech organizations are making state of the art applications and stages that have suggestions across enterprises. From fintech answers for instructive innovations, Jerusalem's tech area mirrors a guarantee to saddling the force of data and innovation for cultural progression.

Computerized reasoning (computer based intelligence), specifically, is a point of convergence of mechanical development in Jerusalem. Specialists at the city's scholastic organizations are pushing the limits of simulated intelligence, investigating applications in normal language handling, PC vision, and AI. Jerusalem's man-made intelligence environment adds to headways in the field as well as makes an interpretation of computer based intelligence examination into viable applications that benefit different areas, from medical care to back.

The city's obligation to development is additionally clear in its drives to cultivate business and backing new companies. Hatcheries, gas pedals, and cooperative work areas give a supporting climate to growing business people to transform their thoughts into feasible undertakings. Jerusalem's startup biological system is different, incorporating a scope of ventures, from biotechnology and medical care to programming improvement and clean energy.

The union of science, medication, and innovation in Jerusalem is maybe most articulated in the domain of advanced wellbeing. The city's specialists and tech trend-setters are at the cutting edge of creating well-being advancements that influence information examination, wearables, and telemedicine. These advancements can possibly change medical care conveyance, making it more customized, open, and proficient.

Furthermore, Jerusalem's headways in clinical innovation stretch out to the improvement of state of the art clinical gadgets and analytic devices. From creative imaging innovations to accuracy clinical instruments, the city's analysts and architects are adding to the development of clinical works on, upgrading diagnostics, and working on understanding results.

The collaboration between the scholarly community, research foundations, and industry in Jerusalem is a critical figure the city's prosperity as a center for science, medication, and innovation. Cooperative drives unite specialists from assorted disciplines, cultivating a climate where thoughts can be shared, and interdisciplinary arrangements can be investigated. This cooperative soul stretches out past the city's boundaries, with worldwide associations intensifying the effect of Jerusalem's commitments on the worldwide stage.

In any case, the way to logical and mechanical progression isn't without challenges. Jerusalem, as other development center points, wrestles with issues, for example, guaranteeing moral practices in research, exploring the intricacies of global cooperation, and addressing differences in admittance to innovation and medical care.

These difficulties require a comprehensive methodology that thinks about the more extensive cultural ramifications of logical and mechanical headways.

Also, the city perceives the significance of supporting the up and coming age of researchers, analysts, and trailblazers. Instructive drives, mentorship projects, and effort endeavors mean to rouse and outfit youthful personalities with the abilities and information expected to add to the city's tradition of advancement. STEM training, specifically, is a point of convergence, guaranteeing that understudies have major areas of strength for an in science, innovation, designing, and math.

All in all, Jerusalem's excursion as a middle for progressions in science, medication, and innovation is a demonstration of its capacity to develop while regarding its verifiable roots. The city's specialists, researchers, and business visionaries are effectively forming the future, adding to worldwide information and development. From archeological disclosures that divulge antiquated secrets to state of the art clinical examination and mechanical arrangements, Jerusalem's effect reverberates across disciplines. As the city keeps on exploring the intricacies of the cutting edge period, its obligation to greatness, coordinated effort, and moral development positions Jerusalem as a guide of progress in a consistently impacting world.

8.3 Discussing the global impact of Jerusalem's contributions to various fields.

Jerusalem, with its significant authentic, social, and strict importance, expands its impact a long ways past its old walls. The city's commitments to different fields have resounded around the world, forming the course of history, propelling information, and impacting assorted parts of human civilization. From strict lessons to logical forward leaps, Jerusalem's effect rises above geological limits, making a permanent imprint on the worldwide stage.

Strictly and socially, Jerusalem holds a focal spot in the convictions of Judaism, Christianity, and Islam. The city's strict importance reaches out past its actual limits, reverberating with a large number of devotees all over the planet. The Western Wall, the Congregation of the Blessed Tomb, and the Vault of the Stone are sacrosanct locales for their separate religions as well as images of a common legacy that joins individuals across mainlands.

The worldwide effect of Jerusalem is maybe most tangible in the domain of otherworldliness and interfaith exchange. Pioneers from different corners of the globe excursion to Jerusalem, looking for otherworldly edification and an association with their strict roots. The city fills in as a gathering point for individuals of various beliefs, encouraging exchange, understanding, and regard among disciples of Judaism, Christianity, and Islam.

Additionally, Jerusalem's social commitments stretch out to writing, workmanship, and music. The city has motivated incalculable works of writing, filling in as a dream for writers, writers, and narrators.

Craftsmen from different customs have portrayed the city's scenes and compositional wonders in their manifestations, catching the embodiment of Jerusalem's persona. Also, the city's assorted social legacy is reflected in its music, with conventional tunes reverberating through its roads and resounding across the world.

In the area of paleontology, Jerusalem's worldwide effect is great. The city's archeological locales, including the Old City and the City of David, have yielded antiquities that offer experiences into antiquated developments. The removal and safeguarding endeavors in Jerusalem set a norm for archeological practices worldwide, impacting the manner in which history specialists and archeologists approach the investigation of the past. The disclosures made in Jerusalem contribute not exclusively to the comprehension of the city's set of experiences yet additionally to more extensive verifiable stories that shape how we might interpret human progress.

Jerusalem's impact in the logical domain reaches out to clinical exploration and medical services. The joint efforts between establishments like the Jewish College of Jerusalem and Hadassah Clinical Center have prompted leap forwards with suggestions for worldwide wellbeing. Research in regions like immunology, hereditary qualities, and regenerative medication has broad results, offering expect worked on clinical medicines and progressions in medical care rehearses around the world.

The city's effect on innovation and development is progressively huge on the worldwide stage. Jerusalem's startup environment, with its emphasis on network safety, computerized reasoning, and biotechnology, adds to headways that rise above public lines. The online protection arrangements created in Jerusalem, for example, address difficulties looked by associations and people around the world, mirroring the city's job as a worldwide player in the innovation area.

Jerusalem's impact in the worldwide field additionally stretches out to strategy and international affairs. The city's status as a point of convergence of political and strict importance has made it a central member in international conversations. The intricacies of the Center East harmony process and the international elements encompassing Jerusalem have suggestions that resound a long ways past the district. Choices and advancements connected with Jerusalem have repercussions for worldwide governmental issues and global relations.

Moreover, Jerusalem's worldwide effect is appeared in its job as a middle for scholarly greatness and examination. The city's colleges, research organizations, and research organizations add to the headway of information in different fields. Joint efforts between Jerusalem-based specialists and their partners all over the planet cultivate a worldwide trade of thoughts, pushing the limits of scholarly request and adding to the aggregate pool of human information.

With regards to natural maintainability, Jerusalem's drives have suggestions for worldwide endeavors to address environmental change and advance eco-accommodating practices. The city's emphasis on water protection innovations, sustainable power, and reasonable metropolitan arranging fills in as a model for other metropolitan communities wrestling with the difficulties of natural corruption. Jerusalem's obligation to feasible practices reverberates around the world, rousing urban areas to take on ecologically cognizant measures.

The city's effect on social legacy safeguarding is one more component of its worldwide impact. Endeavors to defend and advance Jerusalem's social legacy, including computerized chronicles and augmented reality encounters, add to the more extensive talk on saving the social traditions of humankind. As a city with a rich embroidery of history, Jerusalem's undertakings in social legacy conservation set a model for different urban communities with huge verifiable and social resources.

Jerusalem's worldwide effect isn't without challenges. The international intricacies encompassing the city, including the Israeli-Palestinian struggle, have suggestions for provincial steadiness and worldwide harmony. Choices connected with Jerusalem's status resound across the world, with international pressures impacting strategic relations and forming global talk on compromise.

In addition, Jerusalem's worldwide commitments feature the interconnectedness of humankind. The city's impact rises above strict, social, and political partitions, underlining the common legacy of humankind. As an image of solidarity and variety, Jerusalem moves us to perceive our normal humankind and work towards a world described by shared regard, understanding, and coordinated effort.

Jerusalem's commitments to different fields enduringly affect a worldwide scale. From its strict importance to archeological disclosures, logical headways, and social legacy safeguarding, the city's impact resounds across landmasses. Jerusalem fills in as a scaffold between the past and the future, between various religions and societies, and among nearby and worldwide viewpoints. As the city keeps on exploring the intricacies of the cutting edge period, its persevering through inheritance as a worldwide focal point of impact highlights the interconnectedness of our common human experience.

Jerusalem, a city saturated with history and social importance, has caused significant commitments to different fields that to reverberate across the domains of religion, paleohistory, science, medication, and innovation. Its effect stretches out past its old walls, molding the course of human civilization and affecting different parts of worldwide legacy.

Strictly, Jerusalem holds a focal spot in the convictions of Judaism, Christianity, and Islam. The city's importance is implanted in hallowed texts, and its strict milestones are adored by millions around the world.

The Western Wall, a leftover of the Subsequent Sanctuary, is a point of convergence for Jewish supplication and reflection. The Congregation of the Heavenly Mausoleum remains as an image of Christianity, incorporating the site of Jesus' execution and entombment. The Vault of the Stone, a notorious Islamic hallowed place, denotes the spot accepted to be where the Prophet Muhammad rose to paradise.

Jerusalem's commitments to strict idea and philosophy have a significant worldwide effect. The city's part in the Abrahamic beliefs cultivates a feeling of interconnectedness among devotees around the world. Pioneers from various corners of the globe excursion to Jerusalem, looking for otherworldly illumination and an association with their strict roots. The city fills in as a gathering point for individuals of various religions, encouraging exchange, understanding, and regard among followers of Judaism, Christianity, and Islam. Jerusalem, as an image of strict solidarity, impacts the worldwide talk on interfaith relations and advances the possibility of concurrence.

Socially, Jerusalem has been a wellspring of motivation for writing, craftsmanship, and music. The city's rich history, building wonders, and strict importance have enthralled the minds of authors, artists, and writers all through the ages. Artistic works set in Jerusalem frequently investigate subjects of otherworldliness, personality, and the human experience. Craftsmen from different customs have portrayed Jerusalem's scenes and verifiable locales in their manifestations, adding to a worldwide social embroidery that draws motivation from the city's persona.

In the domain of music, Jerusalem's impact is apparent in conventional songs and strict psalms. The city's assorted social legacy, molded by hundreds of years of conjunction among various strict and ethnic networks, is reflected in its melodic customs. Songs resounding through the roads of Jerusalem find reverberations in organizations and exhibitions all over the planet, displaying the city's job as a social signal with worldwide resonations.

Archeologically, Jerusalem remains as an archeological mother lode with destinations, for example, the Old City and the City of David uncovering layers of history going back millennia. The archeological disclosures made in Jerusalem not just develop how we might interpret the city's past yet additionally add to more extensive verifiable accounts that illuminate our understanding regarding antiquated human advancements. The careful unearthing and protection endeavors set a norm for archeological practices internationally, impacting the manner in which history specialists and archeologists approach the investigation of the past.

Jerusalem's archeological commitments have suggestions for worldwide legacy safeguarding. The city's endeavors to uncover and protect verifiable antiques give significant bits of knowledge into antiquated societies and human advancements.

These disclosures add to scholastic exploration as well as improve our aggregate comprehension of humankind's common history. Subsequently, Jerusalem's effect on prehistoric studies rises above nearby and territorial limits, impacting the worldwide account on authentic conservation and social legacy.

Deductively, Jerusalem has been a focal point of scholarly request and revelation since old times. The city's profound authentic roots and scholarly customs have encouraged a climate helpful for logical investigation. Contemporary scientists expand on the establishments laid by their ancestors, adding to progressions with worldwide ramifications.

In the field of natural exploration, Jerusalem's drives have suggestions for worldwide endeavors to address environmental change and advance eco-accommodating practices. The city's emphasis on water preservation innovations, sustainable power, and reasonable metropolitan arranging fills in as a model for other metropolitan habitats wrestling with the difficulties of ecological debasement. Jerusalem's obligation to economical practices reverberates around the world, moving urban communities to embrace naturally cognizant measures.

In the domain of clinical exploration and medical services, Jerusalem's commitments have sweeping ramifications for worldwide wellbeing. Coordinated efforts between organizations like the Jewish College of Jerusalem and Hadassah Clinical Center have prompted leap forwards in regions like immunology, hereditary qualities, and regenerative medication. Jerusalem's examination drives in clinical sciences offer expect worked on clinical medicines and progressions in medical care rehearses around the world.

The city's effect on innovation and development is progressively huge on the worldwide stage. Jerusalem's startup environment, with its attention on network protection, man-made consciousness, and biotechnology, adds to headways that rise above public lines. The online protection arrangements created in Jerusalem, for example, address difficulties looked by associations and people around the world, mirroring the city's job as a worldwide player in the innovation area.

Jerusalem's impact in the worldwide field reaches out to strategy and international relations. The city's status as a point of convergence of political and strict importance has made it a central member in international conversations. The intricacies of the Center East harmony process and the international elements encompassing Jerusalem have suggestions that resound a long ways past the locale. Choices and advancements connected with Jerusalem have repercussions for worldwide governmental issues and global relations.

Additionally, Jerusalem's worldwide commitments feature the interconnectedness of mankind. The city's impact rises above strict, social, and political partitions, stressing the common legacy of mankind.

As an image of solidarity and variety, Jerusalem provokes us to perceive our normal humankind and work towards a world described by common regard, understanding, and cooperation.

The city's effect on social legacy protection is one more element of its worldwide impact. Endeavors to protect and advance Jerusalem's social legacy, including computerized chronicles and augmented reality encounters, add to the more extensive talk on safeguarding the social traditions of humankind. As a city with a rich embroidery of history, Jerusalem's undertakings in social legacy protection set a model for different urban communities with huge verifiable and social resources.

In the field of data innovation and computerized reasoning, Jerusalem's impact is developing. The city's obligation to advancement and business venture has prompted the rise of new businesses and tech organizations that foster state of the art applications and stages. From fintech answers for instructive innovations, Jerusalem's tech area mirrors a pledge to saddling the force of data and innovation for cultural progression.

Man-made brainpower, specifically, is a point of convergence of mechanical development in Jerusalem. Scientists at the city's scholastic foundations are pushing the limits of simulated intelligence, investigating applications in normal language handling, PC vision, and AI. Jerusalem's computer based intelligence biological system adds to progressions in the field as well as makes an interpretation of simulated intelligence examination into down to earth applications that benefit different areas, from medical services to fund.

The union of science, medication, and innovation in Jerusalem is maybe most articulated in the domain of advanced wellbeing. The city's scientists and tech trend-setters are at the bleeding edge of creating wellbeing advances that influence information examination, wearables, and telemedicine. These developments can possibly change medical services conveyance, making it more customized, available, and productive.

Besides, Jerusalem's progressions in clinical innovation reach out to the improvement of state of the art clinical gadgets and analytic apparatuses. From creative imaging innovations to accuracy clinical instruments, the city's specialists and designers are adding to the development of clinical works on, upgrading diagnostics, and working on quiet results.

Jerusalem's worldwide effect isn't without challenges. The international intricacies encompassing the city, including the Israeli-Palestinian struggle, have suggestions for territorial security and worldwide harmony. Choices connected with Jerusalem's status resonate across the world, with international strains affecting conciliatory relations and molding global talk on compromise.

In addition, the city perceives the significance of sustaining the up and coming age of researchers, scientists, and pioneers. Instructive drives, mentorship projects, and effort endeavors plan to motivate and furnish youthful personalities with the abilities and information expected to add to the city's tradition of development. STEM training, specifically, is a point of convergence, guaranteeing that understudies have major areas of strength for an in science, innovation, designing, and math.

The moral components of Jerusalem's commitments to different fields likewise come to the front. As headways in regions like computer based intelligence, biotechnology, and network safety keep on reshaping ventures and social orders, moral contemplations become vital. Guaranteeing that development is directed by standards of decency, straightforwardness, and social obligation is vital for building trust and relieving possible dangers.

9

Chapter 9

Future Prospects and Challenges

What's in store holds a horde of possibilities and difficulties that will shape the course of human life. As we stand at the limit of another time, innovative progressions, cultural changes, and worldwide difficulties loom not too far off. In the domain of innovation, the speed of development keeps on speeding up, promising a future where man-made brainpower, mechanization, and biotechnology will rethink the texture of our regular routines.

Perhaps of the main possibility on the mechanical wilderness is the proceeded with improvement of man-made reasoning (computer based intelligence). Artificial intelligence has proactively taken amazing steps, from self-driving vehicles to remote helpers that can comprehend and answer normal language. The reconciliation of man-made intelligence into different enterprises, like medical services, money, and assembling, holds the commitment of expanded effectiveness, efficiency, and critical thinking abilities. Notwithstanding, the ascent of simulated intelligence additionally delivers moral contemplations and worries about work relocation.

Robotization, firmly connected to simulated intelligence, is another power that will shape the future scene. The arrangement of robots and computerized frameworks in ventures going from assembling to administrations is supposed to alter the manner in which we work. While computerization can prompt expanded productivity and decreased costs for organizations, it likewise represents a danger to occupations generally performed by people. Finding some kind of harmony between mechanical advancement and labor force soundness will be a basic test before long.

Biotechnology is ready to introduce another time of medical care and human increase. Headways in quality altering, customized medication, and regenerative treatments hold the possibility to fix sicknesses that were once viewed as serious. The capacity to change qualities raises moral difficulties, for example, the possibility of "planner infants" and the potential for unseen side-effects. Finding some kind of harmony between logical advancement and moral contemplations will be vital to exploring the fate of biotechnology dependably.

In the domain of room investigation, what's in store holds energizing prospects. Privately owned businesses, powered by aggressive business visionaries like Elon Musk and Jeff Bezos, are driving another space race. The possibility of colonizing different planets, like Mars, is not generally restricted to the domains of sci-fi. Nonetheless, the difficulties of room travel, remembering the actual cost for the human body, strategic obstacles, and ecological manageability, should be defeated to make interplanetary colonization a reality.

The fate of energy is a squeezing worry as the world wrestles with the effect of environmental change. Sustainable power sources, for example, sun oriented and wind power, are acquiring conspicuousness as options in contrast to petroleum derivatives. The progress to a maintainable energy future requires mechanical development as well as a principal shift in cultural mentalities and strategies. Defeating personal stakes in the petroleum derivative industry and executing far and wide changes in energy framework are impressive difficulties that should be tended to.

Cultural changes are likewise unfurling at a quick speed. The continuous advanced insurgency has changed the manner in which we convey, work, and cooperate. The ascent of virtual entertainment has associated individuals across the globe yet has likewise brought about issues like falsehood, cyberbullying, and protection concerns. Exploring the computerized scene requires mechanical arrangements as well as a reexamination of cultural standards and values.

Segment shifts, for example, a maturing populace in many created nations, present difficulties to medical care frameworks and social help structures. The requirement for imaginative arrangements in medical services, senior consideration, and retirement arranging turns out to be progressively critical. Adjusting the necessities of a maturing populace with the yearnings of more youthful ages presents complex cultural difficulties that require insightful preparation and strategy execution.

Worldwide difficulties, for example, pandemics and environmental change, highlight the interconnectedness of the world. The Coronavirus pandemic has featured the weaknesses of worldwide wellbeing frameworks and the requirement for facilitated global reactions to wellbeing emergencies. Environmental change represents an existential danger that requires coordinated endeavors to decrease fossil fuel by-products, adjust to changing ecological circumstances, and alleviate the effect on weak networks.

The international scene is likewise advancing, with moving power elements and the rise of new players on the world stage. Contest for assets, impact, and mechanical matchless quality will characterize worldwide relations before very long. Finding some kind of harmony between public interests and worldwide participation is a fragile errand that requires political expertise and key prescience.

Training is a foundation of cultural advancement, and the eventual fate of learning is going through a change. The customary model of instruction is being tested by web based learning stages, virtual study halls, and intuitive advancements. The openness of data has expanded, however so has the requirement for decisive reasoning abilities and flexibility notwithstanding quickly changing information scenes. Spanning the computerized partition and guaranteeing fair admittance to training will be principal in molding a future where information is a strong power for positive change.

As we explore the intricacies representing things to come, moral contemplations become the dominant focal point. The turn of events and arrangement of new advances bring up significant issues about the moral ramifications of our activities. From the utilization of simulated intelligence in decision-production to the results of hereditary designing, moral systems should be laid out to direct the dependable advancement of innovation. Offsetting development with moral contemplations is a sensitive dance that requires steady carefulness and a pledge to values that focus on the prosperity of mankind.

In the midst of the bunch prospects that what's in store holds, challenges proliferate. One of the focal difficulties is the requirement for manageable improvement that offsets financial development with natural preservation. The exhaustion of regular assets, contamination, and environmental change require a shift towards manageable practices in enterprises, horticulture, and daily existence. Finding some kind of harmony between monetary turn of events and natural stewardship is fundamental for guaranteeing the prosperity of people in the future.

What's in store likewise presents difficulties to the idea of work as far as we might be concerned. Robotization and man-made intelligence can possibly change the idea of occupations, delivering some outdated while setting out new open doors. The ascent of the gig economy and remote work has proactively tested conventional thoughts of business. Adjusting to these progressions requires a reconsideration of instruction and preparing frameworks, social wellbeing nets, and strategies that help an adaptable and dynamic labor force.

Medical services frameworks all over the planet face the double difficulties of propelling clinical science and guaranteeing impartial admittance to mind. While forward leaps in clinical examination hold the commitment of new medicines and fixes, abberations in medical care access continue. What's in store requires a pledge to tending to these disparities, whether they be founded on geology, financial status, or different variables. The mix of innovation into medical services frameworks can assume a significant part in further developing access, productivity, and patient results.

In the domain of administration, what's in store requests imaginative ways to deal with address the intricacies of a quickly impacting world. The ascent of populism, patriotism, and difficulties to popularity based standards highlight the requirement for vigorous establishments that maintain law and order and safeguard majority rule standards. Exploring the convergence of innovation, governmental issues, and morals requires visionary initiative and a pledge to encouraging comprehensive and straightforward administration.

The interconnected idea of worldwide difficulties requires global collaboration on a phenomenal scale. From addressing environmental change to overseeing worldwide wellbeing emergencies, no single country can handle these issues in confinement. Discretion, multilateralism, and the reinforcing of global organizations are fundamental for building a stronger and helpful world.

As we peer into the future, the job of people in forming the course of history turns out to be progressively critical. Our decisions, both as people and as an aggregate society, will decide the direction of human civilization. Moral contemplations, mindful development, and a guarantee to the benefit of everyone should direct our activities as we explore the strange waters representing things to come.

All in all, what's in store is an embroidery woven with the strings of mechanical advancement, cultural change, and worldwide difficulties. The possibilities are enticing, offering the potential for exceptional progressions in science, medication, and human prosperity. Notwithstanding, the difficulties are considerable, requiring smart answers for guarantee a reasonable and fair future. As we stand near the precarious edge of this obscure wilderness, the decisions today will shape the scene of tomorrow. It is an aggregate liability to outline a course that embraces the potential outcomes representing things to come while protecting the qualities that characterize our humankind.

9.1 Discussing the potential future developments and challenges for Jerusalem as a "Holy Hub."

Jerusalem, a city venerated by three significant monotheistic religions - Judaism, Christianity, and Islam - holds a one of a kind and critical spot in the hearts and brains of millions around the world. This antiquated city, with its rich history and strict significance, remains at the junction of expected future turns of events and complex difficulties. The thought of Jerusalem as a "Heavenly Center point" embodies the multi-layered nature of its part in strict, social, and international settings.

Investigating the future, one likely improvement for Jerusalem is the proceeded with development of strict the travel industry. Pioneers from around the world visit Jerusalem to investigate its sacrosanct locales, like the Western Wall, the Congregation of the Blessed Mausoleum, and the Arch of the Stone. As innovation progresses, vivid virtual encounters and expanded reality could upgrade the journey insight, permitting people who can't genuinely go to Jerusalem to draw in with its blessed locales in a significant way. This can possibly make a more comprehensive and internationally associated local area of devotees.

Notwithstanding, the flood in strict the travel industry additionally presents difficulties. Dealing with the flood of guests while safeguarding the holiness of the strict destinations and the personal satisfaction for Jerusalem's inhabitants is a fragile equilibrium. Framework improvement, like transportation and convenience offices, should be painstakingly intended to oblige the developing number of travelers without hurting the authentic and social texture of the city. Finding some kind of harmony requires coordinated effort between strict specialists, city organizers, and neighborhood networks.

Another potential future improvement is the job of Jerusalem as a middle for interfaith discourse and understanding. Given its importance to numerous religions, Jerusalem can possibly act as an unbiased ground for cultivating discussions between various confidence networks. Drives that advance shared regard, resilience, and participation among disciples of various religions could add to a more amicable conjunction.

Be that as it may, accomplishing interfaith agreement in Jerusalem isn't without its difficulties. The city's set of experiences is set apart by strict and political strains, and well established clashes have frequently eclipsed endeavors at discourse. Political contemplations and contending regional cases further muddle endeavors to lay out Jerusalem as a genuine place for interfaith comprehension. Beating these difficulties requires supported responsibility from strict pioneers, political figures, and the worldwide local area to advance a dream of Jerusalem as a city of harmony and solidarity.

The international scene encompassing Jerusalem is a basic consider molding its future. The city has been at the focal point of territorial and global struggles, with contending cases and yearnings from Israel and Palestine. The situation with Jerusalem as the capital of Israel and the potential for a two-state arrangement with East Jerusalem as the capital of a future Palestinian state are focal issues in the Israeli-Palestinian struggle.

The political eventual fate of Jerusalem is intently attached to the more extensive quest for an enduring and only goal to the Israeli-Palestinian struggle. Dealings, strategy, and global commitment will assume significant parts in deciding the city's political status and its capacity to work as a "Blessed Center" that rises above political partitions. The test lies in tracking down an answer that regards the strict and verifiable meaning of Jerusalem while tending to the genuine goals and worries of the two Israelis and Palestinians.

Metropolitan turn of events and framework arranging are key contemplations for Jerusalem's future as a "Heavenly Center point." Safeguarding the city's novel person and verifiable legacy while obliging the requirements of a developing populace is a complicated undertaking. Practical metropolitan preparation, legacy safeguarding, and capable the travel industry the executives are fundamental parts of guaranteeing that Jerusalem stays an energetic and bearable city for occupants and guests the same.

The safeguarding of social legacy is especially vital for a city like Jerusalem, where verifiable and strict locales are intertwined into the metropolitan texture. Finding some kind of harmony among improvement and preservation requires a nuanced approach that includes joint effort between civil specialists, protection specialists, and neighborhood networks. Moreover, guaranteeing that improvement projects benefit all occupants, including underestimated networks, is vital to keeping a feeling of social attachment inside the city.

The difficulties of water shortage and natural maintainability additionally pose a potential threat in Jerusalem's sights. The city, arranged in a locale with restricted water assets, faces the continuous test of giving a satisfactory water supply to its occupants. Reasonable water the board rehearses, for example, effective water system frameworks, water reusing, and public mindfulness crusades, are fundamental for tending to this test. Environmental change further intensifies water shortage issues, making it basic for Jerusalem to take on versatile and naturally cognizant strategies.

Social and segment shifts represent extra difficulties for Jerusalem. The city's assorted populace incorporates Jewish, Muslim, and Christian people group, each with its particular social and strict practices. Adjusting the privileges and interests of these networks while encouraging a feeling of shared personality is fundamental for social congruity. Resolving issues of disparity, separation, and admittance to assets requires a guarantee to civil rights and comprehensive administration.

Training assumes a significant part in molding the eventual fate of Jerusalem as a "Heavenly Center point." Advancing a comprehension of the city's strict and social variety among its occupants and guests is imperative for cultivating resistance and common regard. Instructive drives that feature the common history and interconnectedness of the city's strict networks can add to a feeling of normal legacy.

In any case, training alone can't address the well established political and authentic divisions that continue in Jerusalem. Endeavors to fabricate spans between networks should be supplemented by more extensive cultural changes, including evenhanded strategies, monetary open doors for all, and a pledge to common freedoms. Beating the difficulties of social discontinuity requires an all encompassing methodology that tends to both the quick worries and the fundamental underlying issues.

In the domain of innovation, the eventual fate of Jerusalem as a "Sacred Center point" could see the reconciliation of computerized devices to improve the strict and social experience for guests. Computer generated reality (VR) and expanded reality (AR) applications could offer vivid directed voyages through verifiable destinations, giving setting and data to guests. Moreover, computerized stages could work with interfaith discourse, associating people from various areas of the planet who share an interest in Jerusalem's strict and social legacy.

Notwithstanding, the reception of innovation additionally raises moral contemplations. Adjusting the utilization of computerized devices to improve openness with the need to save the credibility and sacredness of strict locales is a sensitive undertaking. Finding some kind of harmony requires coordinated effort between innovation engineers, strict specialists, and legacy protection specialists to guarantee that mechanical headways contribute decidedly to the city's personality and don't think twice about social respectability.

The monetary fate of Jerusalem is complicatedly attached to its job as a "Blessed Center point." Strict the travel industry, whenever oversaw mindfully, can possibly contribute essentially to the city's economy. Neighborhood organizations, including eateries, lodgings, and high quality shops, stand to profit from the inundation of guests. Notwithstanding, the financial advantages should be disseminated impartially, and measures ought to be set up to forestall the double-dealing of nearby assets for transient increases.

The improvement of feasible and mindful the travel industry rehearses is fundamental for augmenting the positive financial effect while limiting the unfortunate results. Local area based the travel industry drives that enable neighborhood inhabitants and grandstand the bona fide social encounters of Jerusalem can be a mutual benefit for the two guests and the city's economy. In addition, enhancing the monetary base past the travel industry, through interests in innovation, schooling, and development, can add to long haul financial strength.

9.2 Exploring opportunities for further global collaboration and positive impact.

Investigating open doors for additional worldwide joint effort and positive effect is an essential undertaking as the world countenances complex difficulties that rise above public boundaries. In an undeniably interconnected and related worldwide scene, resolving issues, for example, environmental change, general wellbeing emergencies, monetary disparity, and international strains requires aggregate endeavors and cooperative arrangements. This investigation digs into the possible roads for worldwide participation and the positive effect that can be accomplished through cooperative undertakings.

One unmistakable region for worldwide cooperation is environmental change alleviation and feasible turn of events. The criticalness of tending to environmental change has never been more clear, with climbing temperatures, outrageous climate occasions, and ecological corruption presenting huge dangers to the planet. Worldwide collaboration, like the Paris Understanding, mirrors a common obligation to diminishing ozone harming substance discharges and changing toward a practical, low-carbon future.

Growing and developing worldwide joint efforts in environmentally friendly power exploration and execution is a key an open door. Putting resources into clean energy innovations, sharing prescribed procedures, and laying out worldwide systems for feasible energy strategies can speed up the change to a greener worldwide energy scene. Cooperative drives can likewise resolve issues of ecological preservation, biodiversity security, and the economical utilization of normal assets, cultivating an aggregate obligation to saving the planet for people in the future.

General wellbeing crises, as exemplified by the worldwide reaction to the Coronavirus pandemic, highlight the requirement for reinforced global joint effort in medical services. Upgrading worldwide wellbeing foundation, early admonition frameworks, and pandemic readiness requires composed endeavors among countries. Drives that elevate even-handed admittance to immunizations, prescriptions, and medical care assets can add to building a stronger and comprehensive worldwide wellbeing framework.

Additionally, joint effort in logical exploration and development can drive leap forwards in clinical medicines, sickness counteraction, and general wellbeing methodologies. Sharing information, mastery, and assets on a worldwide scale can upgrade our aggregate capacity to answer arising wellbeing dangers and further develop by and large worldwide wellbeing results. By focusing on global cooperation in medical care, countries can add to a better and safer world for all.

Training is a foundation of positive worldwide effect, as it enables people, cultivates understanding, and constructs spans between societies. Reinforcing worldwide participation in training includes drives, for example, understudy trade programs, joint examination projects, and the improvement of universally perceived instructive principles.

By advancing culturally diverse comprehension and cultivating a feeling of worldwide citizenship, training can add to separating boundaries and building an additional interconnected and amicable world.

Mechanical advancement and the computerized upheaval present critical open doors for worldwide cooperation and positive effect. Headways in data innovation, man-made consciousness, and correspondence stages empower continuous cooperation among people and associations across the globe. Utilizing innovation for shared objectives, for example, tending to environmental change, advancing reasonable turn of events, and further developing medical care, can enhance the positive effect of cooperative endeavors.

Worldwide joint efforts in innovation can likewise assume a vital part in spanning the computerized partition. Drives that emphasis on growing web access, advancing computerized education, and encouraging development in underserved districts can add to making a more comprehensive worldwide computerized scene. By guaranteeing that the advantages of mechanical advancement are open to all, worldwide coordinated efforts in the computerized domain can enable networks and drive positive cultural change.

Exchange and financial organizations offer roads for worldwide joint effort that can drive monetary development, work creation, and neediness decrease. Free and fair economic alliance, too as worldwide monetary unions, can work with the progression of merchandise, administrations, and ventures across borders. By eliminating obstructions to exchange, countries can animate financial turn of events, advance development, and improve the general prosperity of their populaces.

Worldwide joint efforts in monetary improvement ought to focus on manageability and inclusivity. Endeavors to address pay disparity, advance civil rights, and execute dependable strategic policies can add to making a more fair worldwide monetary framework. Furthermore, supporting emerging countries in building hearty and economical economies can cultivate more noteworthy steadiness and versatility on a worldwide scale.

Social trade and tact assume urgent parts in advancing shared understanding and cultivating positive connections between countries. Worldwide social joint efforts, like workmanship shows, live performances, and instructive trades, add to building spans between different social orders. These drives work with exchange, challenge generalizations, and advance a feeling of shared humankind.

Discretionary endeavors are fundamental for forestalling and settling clashes, and global associations like the Unified Countries assume a focal part in encouraging discourse and collaboration among countries.

Reinforcing conciliatory ties, advancing compromise components, and maintaining global regulation add to an additional tranquil and stable world. By focusing on exchange over a conflict, countries can cooperate to address normal difficulties and fabricate a safer worldwide climate.

Ecological preservation and biodiversity assurance are basic regions where worldwide cooperation can yield positive results. The corruption of environments, deforestation, and the deficiency of biodiversity are worldwide difficulties that require composed endeavors. Peaceful accords, for example, the Show on Organic Variety, set the system for cooperative activity to save the world's environments and defend the assortment of life on The planet.

Endeavors to battle unlawful natural life exchange, safeguard imperiled species, and advance feasible practices in agribusiness and ranger service can be enhanced through worldwide coordinated effort. By sharing information, assets, and best practices, countries can cooperate to address the underlying drivers of ecological debasement and advance a more supportable connection among mankind and the regular world.

Compassionate guide and fiasco reaction present quick open doors for worldwide cooperation to ease human anguish and give help to impacted networks. Cataclysmic events, clashes, and general wellbeing crises frequently rise above public limits, requiring quick and composed global reactions. Cooperative endeavors in helpful guide include the activation of assets, mastery, and calculated help to address the quick necessities of those impacted.

Also, progressing drives that attention on neediness mitigation, admittance to clean water, and food security add to long haul positive effect. Worldwide coordinated efforts around there include associations between legislatures, non-administrative associations (NGOs), and global offices. By cooperating, the worldwide local area can gain ground toward accomplishing Economical Improvement Objectives and working on the personal satisfaction for weak populaces.

Difficulties to additional worldwide coordinated effort and positive effect are, regardless, imposing. Public interests, international strains, and contending needs among countries can obstruct aggregate activity. Conquering these provokes requires a promise to strategy, discourse, and a common acknowledgment of the interconnectedness of worldwide issues. Worldwide foundations and multilateral systems assume a urgent part in working with collaboration and tending to normal difficulties.

Financial inconsistencies and inconsistent admittance to assets stay critical deterrents to positive worldwide effect. Endeavors to overcome any barrier among well-to-do and non-industrial countries, address pay imbalance, and advance civil rights are fundamental for making a more comprehensive worldwide society.

Worldwide coordinated efforts that focus on the requirements of minimized networks and advance evenhanded dispersion of assets add to an existence where thriving is shared by all.

Besides, the ascent of patriot opinions and protectionist strategies in certain districts represents a test to the soul of worldwide cooperation. Conquering these hindrances requires a recharged obligation to the standards of worldwide collaboration, multilateralism, and the quest for shared objectives. By cultivating a feeling of shared liability regarding the prosperity of mankind, countries can conquer troublesome propensities and turn out together for everyone's benefit.

Moral contemplations likewise assume a vital part in molding the course of worldwide joint efforts. Drives that regard basic freedoms, maintain natural manageability, and focus on civil rights add to positive effect. Guaranteeing that worldwide joint efforts stick to moral standards and advantage all partners is fundamental for building trust and cultivating long haul participation.

9.3 Concluding thoughts on the enduring significance of Jerusalem on the global stage.

Finishing up considerations on the getting through meaning of Jerusalem on the worldwide stage summon examination about the city's significant effect since the beginning of time and its proceeded with reverberation in contemporary international, strict, and social settings. Jerusalem's getting through importance is established in its status as an otherworldly focal point for Judaism, Christianity, and Islam, making it a point of convergence of shared legacy and challenged stories. As we think about the city's past, present, and future, it becomes clear that Jerusalem's significance rises above its actual limits, venturing into the hearts and brains of individuals all over the planet.

The verifiable and strict significance of Jerusalem is profoundly imbued in the shared mindset of billions of adherents. For Jews, the Western Wall remains as a substantial association with old history and the site of the Subsequent Sanctuary. Christians love the Congregation of the Heavenly Mausoleum, denoting the execution and revival of Jesus Christ. Muslims hold the Vault of the Stone and Al-Aqsa Mosque in high regard, as they are related with the Prophet Muhammad's night process.

The getting through meaning of Jerusalem is reflected in the otherworldly journeys made by disciples of these religions. Pioneers from assorted corners of the globe set out on excursions to Jerusalem to implore, reflect, and interface with their confidence's underlying foundations. The city fills in as a sacrosanct space where devotees look for comfort, edification, and a more profound association with their strict legacy. Notwithstanding the difficulties and strains encompassing Jerusalem, its profound charm stays a strong power that draws individuals from various societies and foundations.

Geopolitically, Jerusalem's getting through importance is clear in its status as a point of convergence of territorial and worldwide consideration. The city's political significance is highlighted by its acknowledgment as the capital of Israel and the desires of Palestinians for East Jerusalem to act as the capital of a future Palestinian state. The Israeli-Palestinian struggle, with its center issues revolved around Jerusalem, has molded the elements of the Center East for a really long time.

Jerusalem's international importance stretches out past the Israeli-Palestinian clash, affecting territorial collusions, political relations, and global talk. Countries overall express their situations on Jerusalem, reflecting more extensive international contemplations and collusions. The city's persevering through importance as an international standard features the intricate transaction of history, religion, and political yearnings on the worldwide stage.

Socially, Jerusalem's getting through importance is appeared in artistic expression, writing, and the common social legacy of mankind. Craftsmen, essayists, and artists from different practices draw motivation from Jerusalem, winding around its accounts, images, and scenes into the texture of worldwide culture. The city's immortal charm has been a dream for innovativeness, encouraging a rich embroidery of imaginative articulations that resound across borders.

Writing, both antiquated and current, has frequently tried to catch the substance of Jerusalem. From strict sacred texts to contemporary books, Jerusalem's roads, walls, and milestones have been portrayed as settings for significant human encounters and profound disclosures. The city's social extravagance rises above strict limits, turning into a wellspring of motivation for narrators and specialists who try to investigate the general subjects of personality, confidence, and the human condition.

Jerusalem's engineering wonders, from the Arch of the Stone toward the Western Wall, stand as demonstrations of human resourcefulness and craftsmanship. These designs are not just actual landmarks but rather typify the goals, convictions, and yearnings of previous eras and present. The getting through meaning of Jerusalem in the domain of culture lies in its capacity to summon a feeling of shared humankind, welcoming individuals to see the value in the excellence of variety and the interconnectedness of our worldwide legacy.

As we mull over Jerusalem's getting through importance, it is fundamental to recognize the complicated difficulties that go with its status as a worldwide point of convergence. The city's challenged nature, set apart by verifiable contentions and progressing international pressures, represents a constant test to accomplishing solidness, harmony, and concurrence. The divisions inside and around Jerusalem reflect more extensive issues of character, sway, and the battle for self-assurance.

Endeavors to address the provokes confronting Jerusalem require a promise to discourse, tact, and a certified comprehension of the different viewpoints that join in the city. The yearnings and complaints of all partners, including Israelis, Palestinians, and the worldwide local area, should be considered chasing after practical and just arrangements. Perceiving the significance of Jerusalem's common legacy to different networks is fundamental for encouraging an environment of shared regard and understanding.

All in all, the persevering through meaning of Jerusalem on the worldwide stage is a complex peculiarity that envelops otherworldliness, international relations, and culture. The city's authentic, strict, and social significance resounds across reality, rising above actual lines and reverberating in the hearts of individuals around the world. Jerusalem's getting through importance moves us to explore the intricacies of its challenged history, international elements, and social extravagance with a pledge to encouraging harmony, understanding, and shared mankind.

As we plan ahead, moving toward the getting through meaning of Jerusalem with a feeling of obligation and a dream for an additional comprehensive and amicable world is basic. Jerusalem's job as an image of shared legacy welcomes us to rise above divisions and work towards shared objectives that advance equity, uniformity, and regard for different personalities. In doing as such, we add to a worldwide story that perceives the getting through meaning of Jerusalem not just as a city with verifiable and strict import however as a signal that enlightens the way towards an additional interconnected and caring world.

Jerusalem, with its rich history and various social legacy, involves an interesting put on the worldwide stage. As quite possibly of the most seasoned city on the planet, its importance rises above public lines and reverberates across different strict and social networks. The city's mind boggling embroidery of history, governmental issues, and otherworldliness has made it a point of convergence of global consideration, with continuous discussions and clashes molding its story.

HOLY HUB JERUSALEM_S GLOBAL IMPACT

At the core of Jerusalem's worldwide importance is its job as a sacred city for three significant Abrahamic religions: Judaism, Christianity, and Islam. The Old City, an UNESCO World Legacy Site, embodies the strict variety with its Western Wall, Church of the Heavenly Tomb, and the Vault of the Stone. These consecrated destinations draw a large number of travelers and vacationers, supporting Jerusalem's status as a profound focal point.

Be that as it may, the strict meaning of Jerusalem has likewise been a wellspring of pressure and struggle. The city's set of experiences is set apart by various victories, intrusions, and changes of rulership. The Campaigns, for instance, made a permanent imprint on Jerusalem, as Christian and Muslim powers conflicted for control. This verifiable setting keeps on impacting the contemporary international scene, with contending cases and yearnings muddling endeavors to accomplish an enduring harmony.

In the advanced time, Jerusalem's worldwide unmistakable quality is complicatedly attached to the Israeli-Palestinian clash. The city has been a point of convergence of dispute since the foundation of the Province of Israel in 1948. The situation with Jerusalem has been a significant staying point in harmony talks, with the two Israelis and Palestinians guaranteeing it as their capital. The Unified Countries and different worldwide entertainers have endeavored to intervene, however a thorough goal stays tricky.

The issue of Jerusalem has likewise assumed a huge part in molding discretionary relations in the more extensive Center East. The city's status has been an energizing point for Middle Easterner countries, with many declining to standardize relations with Israel until the subject of Jerusalem is sufficiently tended to. The continuous strain encompassing the city highlights its representative significance in the more extensive Middle Easterner Israeli clash.

Past the strict and international aspects, Jerusalem has an energetic social scene that resounds universally. The city's exhibition halls, displays, and archeological locales draw in researchers and fans the same.

The Israel Gallery, for example, houses an immense assortment of relics that traverses centuries, offering a complete glance at the locale's set of experiences. The mix of old and present day culture in Jerusalem adds a layer of profundity to its worldwide allure.

Jerusalem's worldwide importance is additionally apparent in the domain of global discretion. The city has been the focal point of discretionary endeavors pointed toward settling the Israeli-Palestinian clash. Different harmony drives, including the Oslo Accords and the Camp David Highest point, tried to address the situation with Jerusalem, perceiving its urgent job in accomplishing a feasible and only goal to the contention.

The US, as a central participant in global tact, plays had a critical impact in forming the talk around Jerusalem. The choice by the Trump organization to perceive Jerusalem as the capital of Israel and migrate the U.S. consulate from Tel Aviv to Jerusalem in 2017 was an exceptionally disputable move. It drew analysis from many quarters, including European partners and Middle Easterner countries, who viewed it as prejudicing the result of future exchanges.

On the other hand, the Biden organization has adopted a more nuanced strategy, stressing a pledge to a two-state arrangement while recognizing Israel's on the whole correct to a protected and perceived capital. The U.S. position on Jerusalem keeps on developing, mirroring the mind boggling nature of the city's status and the fragile equilibrium expected in worldwide strategy.

Jerusalem's worldwide standing isn't restricted to political and strict circles; it reaches out into the domains of the scholarly community, innovation, and advancement. The city is home to top notch research organizations and an expanding startup environment.

The Jewish College of Jerusalem, for example, has created Nobel laureates and made huge commitments to different fields. Jerusalem's rise as a center point for development mirrors its versatility and flexibility in the midst of the continuous difficulties it faces.

The travel industry likewise assumes a vital part in extending Jerusalem onto the worldwide stage. Pioneers and explorers from around the world rush to the city to encounter its strict and authentic importance. The lively business sectors, antiquated roads, and different culinary contributions add to the city's charm. In spite of the difficulties presented by political distress, Jerusalem's allure as a vacationer location perseveres, highlighting its immortal fascination.

The city's structural scene further improves its worldwide allure. The juxtaposition of old designs with present day structures makes a visual story that mirrors Jerusalem's dynamic history. From the thin rear entryways of the Old City to the smooth high rises in the new regions, Jerusalem's engineering recounts an account of progression and change, epitomizing the soul of a city that has seen hundreds of years of human civilization.

Jerusalem's job as a social junction is obvious in celebrations and occasions draw specialists, performers, and entertainers from around the world. The Jerusalem Global Film Celebration, for instance, features a different scope of true to life works, cultivating social trade and discourse. These social drives add to Jerusalem's worldwide picture as a city that rises above its international difficulties to embrace the general language of craftsmanship and innovativeness.

The worldwide reverberation of Jerusalem isn't exclusively characterized by its past or present; it reaches out into the domain of writing and media. Endless books, movies, and narratives have investigated the city's multi-layered character, catching the creative mind of crowds around the world. Whether portrayed as a city of contention, a position of profound greatness, or a social blend, Jerusalem's depiction in different types of media shapes the story that contacts worldwide crowds.

In the domain of news coverage, Jerusalem stays a point of convergence for worldwide journalists covering the Center East. The city's essential significance and the continuous contentions in the district guarantee that it includes conspicuously in worldwide news inclusion. Writers announcing from Jerusalem explore the intricacies of the

Israeli-Palestinian clash, giving bits of knowledge and investigation that impact worldwide view of the locale.

The worldwide talk on Jerusalem additionally meets with issues of basic freedoms and civil rights. The effect of the Israeli-Palestinian clash on the occupants of Jerusalem, especially those in East Jerusalem, brings up issues about relocation, admittance to assets, and the more extensive ramifications of political choices on the existences of people. Basic liberties associations and activists frequently feature these issues, adding to the worldwide discussion on equity and value.

Jerusalem's worldwide importance isn't resistant to the difficulties presented by strict radicalism and philosophical partitions. The city has seen demonstrations of brutality and illegal intimidation, further confounding endeavors to accomplish an enduring harmony. The mind boggling exchange of strict intensity, political goals, and verifiable complaints makes an unpredictable blend that resonates past the city's lines, influencing local and worldwide security.